Business Buying Basics

Your Step-By-Step Guide
For Safely Buying A Business

Martin H. Bloom

ROBERT ERDMANN PUBLISHING
SAN MARCOS, CALIFORNIA, U.S.A.

Library of Congress Cataloging-in-Publication Data

Bloom, Martin H.
    Business buying basics : your step-by-step guide for safely buying a business / Martin H. Bloom.
        p.   cm.
    ISBN 0-945339-54-2 (pbk.) : $12.95
    1. Business enterprises--Purchasing.   I. Title
HD2741.B57   1992
658.1'6--dc20   92-3868
                                         CIP

This book is dedicated to my
mother and best friend,
Sophie Bloom

Contents

       Why people buy or sell a business. The price of success.
       Everyday secrets of success. Businesses that sell.
       Examples of business types. How to work with potential
       sellers and handling responses.

       Important Points to Remember. The Three Basic Ele-
       ments. Seller's Discretionary Cash. Value of Fixtures/
       Equipment and Inventory. Value of the Owner's or
       Manager's Services. The Goodwill Multiplier. Formula
       for Calculating Goodwill. Evaluating a Corporation
       Stock Sale. Things Never to Do and Things to Do.
       When a Business Is Priced Properly. Guideline for Buy-
       ing on Terms. Business Pricing Guidelines. Guidelines
       for Specific Types of Businesses. Guidelines for Speci-
       fic Types of Businesses. Terms. Discretionary Cash.

Preface

For many years, businesses have been changing hands. One owner sells and another buys. This book is directed to the buyer and one fundamental question: How do you know what you are buying?

Many people buy on emotion and justify the purchase with factors. But in today's marketplace, there is and should be little or no room for "guessing" and "emotion." If you are planning or thinking about buying a business and have such thoughts as "What am I doing?" "How do I do it safely?" or "What am I risking?" then this book is for you.

Most business buyers are not completely informed as to the realities of buying a business, yet each year over 5 million businesses change hands.

Much has been written for the business seller, but it seems that the business buyer has been overlooked. This is an in- depth yet easy to understand book that will give you insight into, confidence about, and understanding of safely buying future security, dreams, independence, and comforts. The trick is to make the right decisions in buying your business.

This book is the necessary tool combining creative and time-tested strategies as well as proven tactics that will enable you to successfully structure and consummate a business sale.

For the purpose of this process, a *business* is defined as an organized method of producing revenues routinely over a period of time. A business for sale—someone's "pride and joy," his or her "baby" or "lifelong dream"—is therefore only as good as the data used to interpret its viability to you, the new business buyer.

A business value or sale price is subject to change as the market conditions change. Thus a suggested price is valid for only a short time, and a business's value is relative to the size and scale of a given business in a given class and industry.

The concepts in this book are important. They will make you "street smart" and help ensure your future—all by showing you how to gather the right information.

About the Author

As the owner of a long-standing, successful business marketing and brokerage firm, I have a broad and varied background in business marketing, business sales, mergers, and acquisitions. I have successfully applied my skills nationally on behalf of individual buyers and sellers as well as major corporations.

This book had been written with a commitment and dedication to the business buyer. I have recognized that people who want to accomplish a goal and make a "great business deal" should have a guide specifically oriented to the business buyer. This book is that guide. It takes the business buyer from the beginning of the trip to its successful conclusion: the buying of a business that will be the source of lifelong independence, total security, and control over one's own destiny.

I am pleased to invite you to enter the fascinating world of the entrepreneur. I encourage you to read and absorb all of the details in this book. These are details that have taken many years to develop, and for the first time they are available to you, the new business buyer. My goal is to help you see clearly the path you are on—and to help you safely make the decision to buy the business that will positively change your life and your way of living forever.

1

Beginning the Planning Process

Owning a business has probably been the lifelong dream of almost everyone at one time or another. We tend to think of a business as an expression of autonomy, an independent way of life, and a source of financial freedom.

If you are a free-thinking entrepreneur waiting in the wings for the right moment to buy a business, consider and believe this: Your moment has come. "Whatever you imagine and sincerely desire, whatever you totally believe in and ardently act upon must come to pass." These are the words of a prominent educator, Paul J. Meyer. The importance of self- understanding and annunciation is paramount before you venture into the marketplace to buy a business. Yes, if all your goals, understanding, and analysis are on target, then by all means venture forth and proceed with your dream. But beware that many who have tested the waters for the first time have found them to be cold and harsh.

Naturally, you want to make your entry into the ranks of business owners as painless as possible. First, you must try to get a clear understanding of yourself as a potential business buyer. Ask yourself, "Who am I?" You are special; there has never been another you. This self-understanding is the basis for goal direction. Then ask yourself an additional question: "Do I have what it takes to venture into business ownership? Or am I one of the many who talks about it, dreams about it, but somehow never gets around to taking that first big step?" Be true to yourself and answer honestly. It won't hurt you to face yourself at this point, because you haven't put up any money. But when you do, you should have your eyes wide open and have a sense of informed commitment.

Now let's talk about success. Success is the progressive realization of worthwhile, predetermined, personal goals. It is a continuous journey. You are taking action at all times on this journey. The journey must also be meaningful in order to achieve your overall goal, which is to own a business. Finally, to succeed you must understand the most important factor: It is up to you as an individual to make your success a reality.

The first step for the budding entrepreneur is goal setting. Mark Twain once said, "Everybody talks about the weather, but nobody does anything about it." The same observation can be made about success. Everybody talks about it, but far too few do anything to ensure their own personal success. The reason is improper goal setting. Remember, a goal is simply an end or an objective. It is basic human nature to achieve and accomplish, to do, to attain. Motivation helps us achieve our goals.

Let's consider goals from a business point of view. One thing all businesses have in common is the goal of making a profit and making an impact on competitors or customers. The goal of business has always been to provide a return to owners or stockholders.

Now that we've talked about goals, let's consider you. Are you getting your fair share of the pie, or are you just, like many others, a cog in the giant wheel of business? Many people hire on with an organization and become trapped by their own personal needs. They can't get off the "cart" because their present lifestyle would be threatened without a regular paycheck. Let's face facts: Your security in a job is only as close or as far away as your next paycheck. Your reward is a salary but probably never a piece of the pie. If you don't have control of your destiny, you are a pawn to a system that can't be beat. You may as well just go along for the ride, because chances are you will never be the driver.

Is your job a positive or negative experience? Many budding entrepreneurs find a job stultifying. They resent having to put up with a boss and finding that they are getting more dependent on the job as each year goes by. They start realizing that the job restricts their freedom and reward and is a major cause of negative stress.

On the other hand, the rewards of business ownership—not just any business, but your special business—are many. At this point, settle back in a comfortable chair and close your eyes. Think about the business you always wanted, and picture yourself in that business. Now consider yourself as an independent businessperson, able to be as creative as you want to be, with unlimited potential for income and success. Imagine yourself facing the challenges as the captain of the ship and achieving the grand successes you're imagining with a sense of freedom you've never felt before.

Almost 80% of the work force are employed by others; only 20% own their own business. It's your choice: Follow or lead. Success is attained by those who can master the proper business philosophy, which is to work smart, develop positive attitudes, and set and achieve personal goals. Find a proven system for your venture. It isn't necessary to reinvent the wheel. Attitudes are a learned behavior. Why not start out with positive expectations? Again, if your personal goals are clear enough, then the "how to's" fall into place.

So far, your total investment in the process of buying a business has been your time, to seek a positive and realistic outlook about yourself and a positive and realistic view of what your dream can be. An investment can be either personal or monetary. In either case, you can only evaluate it by the return on the investment (time or money). In short, you can expect to get back something only to the extent that you've put something in.

Have you ever really considered your true feelings and emotions and the part they play in the buying process? Attitudes are learned and not inborn. Then why should you consider an attitude change? If you truly believe "you can't" accomplish a goal, then you can also believe that "you can." What can you change, and what can't you change? You cannot change such external factors as the outdoor temperature and rain. What you can change is your attitude toward those externals. We all have the power of choice. How can we change attitudes, and what controls the results? Our actions. What, then, controls actions? Feelings. What controls feelings? Attitudes. Therefore, an attitude is a learned behavior over which you have total control as long as you recognize what you are trying to accomplish. Your thoughts control your attitudes.

Remember this equation:

Input + Thoughts + Attitudes + Feelings + Actions

= Results (positive or negative)

What determines whether the result is positive or negative is the input. The results are directly in proportion to the law of displacement in which Good in = Good out.

In a study on the nation's population, David McClennan found that only 3 percent were financially independent, 10 percent lived in comfort, 60 percent lived paycheck to paycheck and at retirement lived on Social Security, and 27 percent needed help to live. The 3 percent who were financially independent outperformed the 10 percent who merely lived in comfort by a ratio of 10 to 1 financially. The main difference between the two groups was the roadmap, the goal orientation and positive attitudes, that guided their lives.

The financially independent 3 percent had the "total person concept" to help guide their lives. They allowed positive factors to impact their lives on a daily basis. They succeeded because they made the following elements a part of their daily life:

Physical and health
Mental and education
Family and home
Spiritual and ethical
Social and cultural
Financial and career

If you don't know where you are going, then any road will get you there. To truly succeed, you must have the dedication and willingness to pay the price. To truly succeed, you must have determination. Most people don't win because winners have to push themselves positively each and every day. Most people, when they start to backslide, quit and feel sorry for themselves—which, in reality, is a poor form of release from the daily pressure of keeping up. You win by concentration and visualization, by having courage and the ability to withstand pressure. You win by developing a winning attitude. These are the qualities of successful people: positive mental attitudes, goal direction, and self-motivation. That's the secret of the 3 percent group. They attained so much more just by doing a little bit better than the rest of society, through dedication, concentration, visualization, and push.

If you don't expect to win, then you expect to lose. Remember that, in life, first place is the only place. All others are forgotten. Goals are the objectives of life. Remember to set your imagination free. Have the courage to set and achievel your goals. Visualize along the way. Affirm your convictions by the power of affirmation. Always plan with positive expectancy.

Don't procrastinate either; procrastination is suicide on the installment plan. Do it smart, but do it today. Your biggest gift is time. Don't waste it, for time is money.

Only a little more effort will achieve quantum results. Consider the following. In the game of baseball, the difference between a .200 hitter and a .300 hitter is only one more hit in every ten times at bat. The big difference, however, is that the .200 hitter makes $100,000 per year and the .300 hitter makes $1 million per year. People never use more than 10 to 20 percent of their ability. Everyone has the potential to succeed, but few use it. However, those who do use it can reap wealth, security, satisfaction, peace of mind, and personal growth.

Have a goal, because without it you don't need wealth.

The ability to manage yourself may be the single greatest factor in promoting your business venture. Whether you make the business successful and attain the degree of wealth you desire is solely up to you. The future is yours.

Before you can start to make any long-range plans, you must determine how well you have done and how well you are doing. What you are in today's market is the result of all your yesterdays. What you become tomorrow is simply a reflection of what you are today. Once you systematically work yourself into a satisfactory level of self-understanding, you will be adding to your success and income as well as your attainment of all your personal goals. An honest self-appraisal will really help you.

Try as hard as you can to see yourself from a totally objective point of view, possibly from the point of view that the world sees you. This self-appraisal could either be a positive starting point or just one more time to hide behind dark glasses and avoid the truth. Try, try, try to honestly appraise yourself. This is the most critical point in setting the proper foundation for the "building" you are trying to construct. Go to a mirror, and take along a tape recorder. Look yourself squarely in the eye, and tell yourself how you really feel about yourself. Be honest, be alone, and be true to yourself. Look for the flaws as you listen to your self- critique. Think about what you say, why you say it, and how you will correct those obvious flaws. Everything you say becomes a building block for your future success, not only as a person but also as a self-confident business owner. Those who constantly reexamine themselves to see how they cann upgrade their effectiveness are those who look upon themselves as entrepreneurs who will succeed in attaining their personal and business goals. They are now following the same pattern as successful business owners who steadily increase both their self-esteem and their personal wealth.

Let's digress slightly and examine the reality of your chosen business. A new wall is now erected in front of you. What business are we talking about? Your business, of course. Again close your eyes, sit back in a quiet room, take a deep breath, and think of the type of business you would like to own. It's OK to start with what you think you know best, your present job or career. But soon you will be wandering through the vast reaches of the business community and examining different businesses. How about a flower shop, a manufacturing business, a travel agency? Don't be surprised if your answer is "I don't know what business I want. I just know that I want my own business." Do you feel panic or fear? Is this a major stumbling block? No, this answer just indicates that you must once again sit back and search yourself for the real answer.

It isn't immmortant at this point to know the exact business you want. What is important is that you continue to explore. In ancient Greece, a noble and wise philosopher was known to carry a lantern with him in broad daylight, searching for the truth. He would say that "the only reason we have two ears and just one tongue is so that we may hear more and speak less." These words of wisdom are priceless, especially for struggling entrepreneurs who want insight into themselves, the business world, and everything mentioned thus far. Many people can talk themselves out of succeeding and advancing because they fear the unknown of tomorrow and fall back on the pseudocomforts of today. On the other hand, top-notch candidates for success and advancement know how to listen to themselves and go on to bigger and better things with the positive construction of affirmative personal goals.

Those who are "going for the gold" see things through to completion. They know that the big success requires a series of positive little successes. Just as persistence pays off, so too does planning. Knowing this, goal-directed individuals plan and systematically update their strategy. They realize that each effort or accomplishment holds promise for future success. Positive goal direciton is the ability to see one's efforts clearly and to follow up those efforts with additional positive input that will ensure satisfactory and profitable results. The result is permanent and increasing personal and business success. To attain that level of self-understanding and positively set down short- and long-range goals, you must make a realistic self-appraisal of your abilities. You must at all times strive to improve your positive mental attitude.

Before you retire for the evening, try reviewing the day's activities. Instead of being satisfied with your performance, probe your failures and learn why you were unable to accomplish a particular task or goal. As with everything in life—your profession, your thought, or your ability to get on life's future track—there is no standing still. Whether you get ahead or fall back is your decision to make. The time to make it is right now. Self-evaluate, and learn from your successes and your failures.

Think about a group of people. Ask yourself, "Why will some succeed and some fail? Where will I fail?" Why not ensure your position? A slight edge affords quantum success. Did you ever wonder why a group of salespeople starting out with the same equipment, the same products, the same price list don't all succeed? Why do some fail? The difference is clear: The achievers learn to manage themselves and their products and thereby ensure their future.

Not knowing how to make the most profitable use of one's time is more often responsible for poor performance than even mediocre ability. How well you manage your time will determine the extent of your success in achieving your goals. Understand well the statement "Time waits for no man." All people are equal in the time they have available to achieve their desired goal. All people are equal in the time they have available to achieve their desired goal. Those who make the most use of the time given are the ones who value that time. They don't squander it on useless activity. They know that every minute, every hour added to the positive pursuit of their goals increases their chances of accomplishing those goals. The sooner you realize how to spend your day wisely, that much sooner you will be managing your time for better results and that much sooner you will achieve your ultimate goal. You will be able to easily distinguish between activities that take up too much time and those positive activities that need more time. Record in a small diary your daily activities. After a short period, you'll be able to see where your time is valuable and where you are wasting your time. Again, be honest with yourself and be critical. Get time and activity under control, and you're well on your way to achieving your goal.

Time really is your most valuable asset. Yet the average person spends well over a quarter of the day in activities that do not help achieve his or her goal. Friendly conversation is fine, but meaningless chitchat is simply a waste of valuable time. If you eliminate the waste, you can fill the time with positive, self-fulfilling productivity. The following checklist can help you understand your positives and your negatives in relation to time:

Do I get started after 10 a.m. very often?

Do I spend too much time reading newspapers or just watching television?

Do I simply waste time hanging around home?

Do I waste time wondering what to do, who to see, where to go?

Do I spend too much time on phone conversations that don't achieve results?

Do I waste time by needlessly prolonging meetings?

Do I waste time in inactivity, such as daydreaming?

Do I waste time prolonging conversations?

Do I waste too much time with people who cannot help me accomplish my goals?

Do I spend too much time on personal visits for purposes that could be handled on the telephone?

Do I waste time going to places that have nothing to do with my purposes?

The effective management of your time, funneled toward positive goal direction, will help you discover your dreams: the beginning of your first step toward business ownership and positive attainment of our goal.

Have you ever considered that a person's inability to go forward may stem from his or her inability to overcome self- objections? Bringing up self-objections means, in effect, asking yourself for more reasons to do something. For example, you may be asking yourself to be convinced why you should buy a particular business. A well-prepared and self- informed person should welcome objections when they are raised, not merely discard them as obvious negatives that cannot be overcome. A negative may just prevent you from researching your positive goal. But consider that the road to success starts only when the first resistance is raised. Encourage objections, for in answering them correctly you get closer to your goal. Perhaps you are afraid of the future and not comfortable about being able to handle self-objections, better known as doubt. Most situations don't generate easy objections that are quickly answered. Objections and resistance might turn up at any time, and you must be able to do more than meet them head on. You must be able to formulate a positive answer.

At this time I'd like you to imagine that you have found a business that meets your requirements in all respects except for price. Price is a consideration for one obvious reason: what you can afford. But price can also be viewed from a position of value: "Your price is too high." How about "Your prices are too low"? Have you ever heard anyone say that to a seller? I never did. Nevertheless, a person buying a business that is either considered too expensive or too cheap now has a problem with that business. The buyer has to consider whether an inexpensive business is inferior and therefore priced that low or whether a "quality" business is priced too high. In either case, the price is an objection to overcome.

Objections are always relative. To one person, a business may be worth thousands more than to another person. It could even be priceless. To another person, the same business could be worthless, no matter how low the purchase price may be. Any price is too high until a buyer understands the value he or she is receiving.

View each potential purchase of a business as a balance, positives to the right and negatives to the left. You can look at the scale as one side being price (minuses) and the other side being value (pluses). Build each side carefully by understanding each facet of the prospective business. If all goes to the right (pluses rather than minuses), as we would hope, the value far outweighs what you may have considered a high price. Price then moves to a lower level of priority in your decision about whether or not to buy that particular business. If the weights on both sides of the scale are equal and you have a balance, you obviously have a rougher decision to make than if one side outweighs the other. Keep this balanced scale in mind as you proceed to overcome self-objections. As you overcome your own objections and move weights from the negative column, you may find that the added value overcomes the high price. Then you have found the right business. Again, don't be premature in judging your compilation of facts. Gather all that you can and then see where the scale reads before you make a decision.

If you, as the prospective buyer, feel that a business is too high priced, you are generally wondering, Why is it worth what the seller is asking me to pay? You are also saying to yourself, Show me why I should buy your business. In essence, what you are really saying is that the seller has not shown you or convinced you that there are enough values or benefits in the business to justify what you consider a high price. In that case, try to find out what the benefits and values are so you can come closer to making the decision between purchasing the business and just walking away from it.

There are various ways of finding out the values and benefits of a business. One is simply viewing the business you are thinking of buying against comparable businesses in a similar location. You must go through an exhaustive and time- consuming analysis of the other business, but the effort will pay off in the end if you find out that the business you are thinking of buying is either superior, equal, or inferior to your test model. The important feature in your test case should be the ability of the business to provide superior quality and above-average profits.

Quality is a reflection of the attitudes of the company's management. Although people don't like paying higher prices for goods or services, they invariably come to appreciate quality. Price becomes a secondary matter. As a prospective buyer, always think of quality as the sum of the characteristics that make the goods or services a superior value. When you do this, you are less likely to argue that the quality is too good. Translate that viewpoint to your prospective customers after you take over the business, and observe your customers' reactions to your goods or services. If you provide a top-notch, quality product with competitive prices, you can't miss becoming a success. The old adage states that you get what you pay for. In the short term or over the long haul, you will get much more benefit, dollar for dollar, if you select the company with superior value.

Objections on your part are healthy. As a buyer, you have to know all there is to know, because you don't have the benefit of a crystal ball. The following rational objections are important to understand:

You, the buyer, want to make certain that the business product or service will meet your requirements. You are not objecting but merely aiming at reaching a decision.

You need complete elaboration, clarification, and confirmation of each point of the business—especially those points that are still "gray." Ask more questions, and give yourself the reasons why you should buy this particular business. Good buyers bring up objections because they know that the objections may turn into the very reasons for buying, or rejecting, a prospective business.

The more valid the objection, the better the opportunity for you to receive the logical answer. If an objection is arbitrary, then you will never end up with a valid answer. But if, for instance, your objection is the asking price, then you have the basis for the development of fundamental negotiations. If you cannot afford the asking price, you might ask for terms and conditions of sale that will suit your needs. The seller will then be in a position to consider his or her needs and desires. Remember this: To make a deal, both the seller and the buyer must be willing to negotiate. Above all, they must be reasonable and flexible. The compromises must eventually be perceived as equal for both, or no deal will be struck.

You may now be in a position to purchase a business, but don't do it at this point. The seller would like a commitment from you, but you want time. You are not objecting to buying the business—your objection is buying now. You may tell the seller that you are gathering the information that will enable you to purchase the business but that you need the time to support the information with additional facts. You have now put an additional burden on the seller to give additional information, provided there is additional information to give. You may well be at the critical decision-making point.

Now that you are at the basic point of making a "go" or "no go" decision, I have just a few more ideas for you to consider before we delve into the actual mechanics of buying that special business you've always wanted. In the March 1987 issue of *Nation's Business,* an article titled "A Pre-Flight Checklist" asked this question of future entrepreneurs: Do you really want to leave the corporate nest for independent life? In the following lists, put a check next to any statement that describes your thinking. If the checks under Drawbacks outnumber the checks under Benefits, security is probably more important to you than autonomy. You may be happier staying where you are.

Benefits of Autonomy

( ) Make more money
( ) Work when you please
( ) Work at home
( ) Make independent decisions
( ) Be a big fish in a little pond
( ) Not have to contend with co-workers
( ) Flexibility to compete
( ) Take risks and reap reward
( ) Save on taxes
( ) Not have to cater to boss
( ) Do as you please
( ) Pick your own projects
( ) Be free from boredom

Drawbacks of Autonomy

( ) Get no regular paycheck
( ) Work longer hours
( ) Have to supply your own office
( ) Have nobody to bounce ideas off of
( ) Feel loneliness
( ) Not have financial resources of a large corporation
( ) Suffer personal financial loss if the business fails
( ) Have no corporate perks or benefits
( ) Must answer directly to clients
( ) Be responsible for running a company
( ) Must be motivated to work without supervision
( ) Work hectic, demanding schedule
( ) Miss being in a big pond

While we are in the final phase of self-examination, let's bring into play some questions that only you as the potential buyer can answer, based on your personal and financial needs. For you to locate the "right business," it is important that you really know as much as possible regarding your needs, background, likes and dislikes, interests, and goals. You need to assemble enough information to find the business that you would enjoy owning. Many people do not know the kind of business they want. You can be well on your way to matching your requirements with a business that is available by asking or answering the following questions:

Buyer's Self-Appraisal

Do you plan to operate the business by yourself?

Does your spouse work?

Will other people be financially involved in your business?

How long have you been looking for a business?

What businesses have you looked at?

Why didn't you buy them?

What are or were the responsibilities of your last or current job?

What is or was the extent of your authority?

How long were you employed?

What did you or do you like about the job?

What did you or do you dislike about the job?

Have you ever owned a business? If so, what type? Was it successful? If it was not successful, why not?

What income is needed to maintain your lifestyle?

How much money do you have to invest in a personal business?

Does that figure include working capital?

How liquid is this money?

How long would it take to turn your equity into cash?

Are you willing to wait that long?

If you are depending on a loan, have you applied for one yet?

Are you concerned about the location of the business you buy?

How soon do you want to buy a business?

Is there a type of business you would not consider buying under any circumstances?

If you have taken the time to honestly answer these questions above, you can proceed with the process of finding the right business for you.

2

"The American Dream"

Owning your own business continues to be a critically important personal goal for millions of Amricans and foreign investors. People feel the need to escape the nonidentity of the corporate maze, the stagnation in bureaucracy, and the 8-to-5 cycle. There are approximately 22 million businesses in the United States, and one out of five changes ownership every year. Those that change hands represent a wide spectrum from "mom and pop" stores to large national manufacturing and distributing corporations.

The information contained in this publication constitutes proven techniques providing you, the business buyer, with the required means to successfully structure and consummate a business purchase. The techniques work. Use them precisely as they are presented, and you will be successful.

Why People Buy or Sell a Business

Most of a buyer's or seller's motivation is internal or emotionally driven. These are some of their reasons for making a change:

Sellers	Buyers
Retirement	Upgrade of business
Illness	Recent arrival in area
Relocation	Need for a job
Upgrade of business	Entrepreneurship
Dispute (with partner	Need to avoid transfer
or spouse)	Money and freedom
Inability to handle business	Inheritance
Weariness or boredom (tired of business)	

The Price of Success

Consider two people, both in reasonably good health and both with similar backgrounds, equal talent, the same opportunity, and an expressed desire to succeed. Have you ever wondered why one may fail and the other succeed?

People who fail in their job, career, or business may talk about success and dream about success, but they do very little to achieve it. They yearn but they will not earn. Hence there is always room at the top. Many people are willing to pay the price of climbing the stairway to success, step by step. They often want to start at the top, or they attempt to reach it without the hard work and struggle that is inherent in achieving success.

People who fail have one thing in common: They are primarily interested in enjoying themselves rather than in realizing the final accomplishments. Leisure activities, unproductive pastimes, and countless hours of idle conversation and daydreaming are their way of life.

Successful people are just the opposite. They are more intersted in pleasing results. They have defined success for themselves, they understand what is required to achieve that success, and above all they possess the desire and the persistence to achieve it. They are willing to put forth the effort necessary to reach their goals, even if the required process is less than pleasing.

Success depends on one's understanding of the price that must be paid for success and on one's willingness to pay that price.

The prizes of life are at the end of each journey, not near the beginning. And nobody can know at the beginning how many steps are necessary to reach the goal. Failure may still be encountered at the thousandth step, yet success hides behind the next bend in the road. Nobody ever knows how close success lies without turning the corner.

Everyday Secrets of Success

Fill your day, every day, with appointments with sellers of businesses. If you don't have appointments, you should spend your day canvassing or calling business owners. If you are active in canvassing or calling during the first part of the week, then the later part of the week should be completely taken up with appointments. Businesses for sale can be found in Business Opportunity sections of newspapers (such as the *Los Angeles Times, Washington Post, New York Times, Wall Street Journal,* and countless others), in the listings of professional business opportunity brokers, through personal sources (word of mouth), in the Yellow Pages for various cities, and in business journals, magazines, and industry business guides (all available at your local library's reference desk). If you work at the job of buying a business, setting and keeping appointments, you will find the right business for you.

One of the most important tools is the telephone. You must learn to use it properly, and you must not hesitate to use it. If you are afraid to pick up the phone and make a call and cannot overcome your fear, you will never be able to "reach out and touch someone."

For most of us, the biggest obstacle to success is our fear of rejection. The key to handling rejection is to change your attitude about it. Look at your telephone calls as a method of explorations that take you through a maze of uncharted territory, fill your head with information, and let you develop a map to your goal—the buying of your business.

The phone should be used primarily to arrange appointments. It should not be used to buy a business. Telephone calls should be short and to the point. For instance, when you are talking to the owner of a business who starts questioning you, simply be courteous, state your interest, and ask for an appointment. Once you get together with potential sellers, you must gain their confidence so they will feel comfortable with you as a potential buyer, especially if they are going to carry back a sizable note. All your conversations and interactions with potential sellers should therefore be of a positive nature. Never knock or criticize a business you are investigating in any way. If you do, you will lower that seller's confidence in you and may make him or her reluctant to accept your offer.

Don't hesitate to work hard (nights and weekends) to try and put a deal together. Time is your greatest enemy. When you make an offer, every day and every hour that passes makes the seller less determined to sell you the business. Remember, the seller is continually getting advice from business associates, friends, and relatives—all of whom are pointing out the negatives of your deal. The longer thenegotiations continue, the less motivated the seller becomes. So conclude your negotiations as rapidly as possible, even if you must work nights and weekends. Don't let your deal die from a fatal case of seller's remorse.

You must have the desire and organization to achieve your goals. Write down your goals on paper, update them, and see what you must do to achieve them. Each week, review your progress. Make every effort to achieve your goal through good work habits. Once acquired, good work habits are not easily lost. Devote yourself to the business of buying a business.

Businesses That Sell

Of the estimated 22 million businesses in the United States today, over 90 percent of them gross less than $375,000 annually and have fewer than twelve employees. These are all classified as small businesses, but they vary widely. Here are some of the types of businesses that you as a buyer may find for sale:

Bars and Taverns:	All businesses where alcoholic beverages are consumed on the premises and where food, if any, is not the primary function of the business. Include bars, night clubs, neighborhood taverns, and discos.
Package Liquor Stores:	All businesses selling alcoholic beverages for off-premise consumption. Include liquor distributors, package stores, and liquor stores.
Fast-food Restaurants:	All businesses where food "to go" is the primary function of the business, regardless of the type of food offered. Include fast-food franchises, sandwich shops, shops selling seafood, burgers, and the like to go, specialty takeout restaurants, and "roach coaches" (mobile catering units).
Restaurants:	All businesses serving food not considered "to go." May serve alcoholic beverages, but the prime function is food service. Include breakfast and lunch establishments, such as luncheonettes, delis, soup and salad bars, and cafeterias; as well as dinner establishments, cafes, bar-and-grill combinations, and delis serving dinner.
Other food businesses:	All businesses concentrating on a particular area of food service, such as burgers, ice cream, ethnic foods (such as Mexican or Chinese), donut shops, snack stands, novelty food operations, bakeries, sandwich shops, specialty food shops (cookies, cheese, and the like), and dietetic and gourmet shops.
Markets:	All food operations where food is not normally consumed on the premises, such as grocery stores, convenience markets, drive-through dairies, and delis. May or may not sell alcoholic beverages.
Cleaning operations:	All businesses specializing in the cleaning and washing of garments, such as coin-operated laundries, Laundromats, drop shops (small dry-cleaning shops with no plant), dry-cleaning plants, and pick-up stations.

Service businesses:	All businesses primarily providing services to the public, such as travel agencies, employment services, frame shops, tuxedo rental shops, video sales/rental shops, car washes, massage parlors, dating services, answering services, health and fitness clubs, limousine services, photo-processing shops, print shops, postal services, hair salons, auto services (repair, gasoline, parts), real estate agencies, janitorial services, vending companies, and swimming pool services—among many others.
Retailers:	All businesses that primarily sell products to the public. Include gift shops, bike shops, clothing stores, music stores, flower shops, card shops, tobacco shops, hobby shops, stationery stores, pet shops, hardware stores, book shops, specialty business (silk flowers, fishing and hunting), newsstands, and electronics shops (stereos, computers).
Franchises:	All new franchise offered to the public.
Manufacturers:	All businesses that produce a product
Distributors:	All businesses that sell manufactured goods produced by others. They sell primarily to retailers or manufacturers for producing additional goods.
Miscellaneous:	All businesses that do not logically fit any other category.

How to Work with Potential Sellers and Handling Responses

Let's say that you have made up your mind as to the exact type of business you would like to own. Now what? You could read the Business Opportunity sections of newspapers and call about interesting listings, call a business boker, ask friends, or take any other reasonable approach to finding your "ideal" business. But none of these approaches gives you control— and control is the name of the game. You have to know firsthand anything and everything about the business that you want to buy. Without information concerning finances, employees, market share, trends, and so on, you remain in the dark. Stay in the sunshine, and glean everything about the business so you can make an informed decision and have an excellent chance of success.

Information gathering is covered later on. For now, let's concentrate on dealing directly with the business owners whom you found in your search for that perfect, profitable business. In dealing with these sellers, listen to what is really being said. Listen carefully to each of their responses. Did an owner say yes or maybe? In buying a business, there are few real noes, because a no may change. Answers can be had, objections overcome by softening the owner's response, asking a qualifying question, and helping the owner provide the right answer.

Above all, always be courteous, friendly, confident, and affirmative. Don't be hesitant.

Let's work with some real-life situations. Imagine that you are the buyer, brokering your own business. The following suggestions include a statement to soften the owner's response, a qualifying question, and action to take.

Owner Says	You Say	
"I'm doing great, I'm making all kinds of money. I wouldn't consider selling."	**Soften:**	"You really have a nice business. I can see you are doing well."
	Qualify:	"If you did decide to sell, when would be the best time—at the peak or on the decline?"
	Take action:	Help the owner understand that the best time to sell a business for maximum return is when it's doing well. If he or she still says no, get a referral to a competitor, similar businesses in the area, or friends. Always check back later. Leave your name and telephone number and be sure to check back when you said you would.

"I've been giving some thought to selling."	**Soften:**	"Good, now is the ideal time to sell. I would like to explore the possbility of buying your business. What do you think?"
	Qualify:	"What are you planning to do after your sell your business?"
	Take action:	Help the owner understand that now is a good time to start selling the business. Find out the reason he or she was thinking about it. Then build on those reasons.
"I'll sell, but I want all cash."	**Soften:**	"I can understand your desire for an all-cash offer."
	Qualify:	"What you are really asking is, if you did sell on terms, would you really receive your money."
	Take action:	Help the seller understand that the two of you can put together a program that works. Ask the seller, "If we could put together a program that would produce virtually a zero foreclosure rate, would you consider selling on terms?" Point out the limitations of an all-cash deal: the tax bite to the seller, the scarcity of buyers who have that kind of money to put down, a buyer's need for working capital, without which the business would fail.
"Everything I have is for sale."	**Soften:**	"That's great! However, the only thing I'm interested in buying is your business."
	Qualify:	"When can we sit down to seriously discuss my buying your business?"
	Take action:	Find out how serious the owner is. Does he or she have a reason to sell? Help the owner understand what is realistic in selling the business.

"Yes, I want to sell my business." **Soften:** "That's great!"

Qualify: "Let's get together to discuss your business and see how we both can be satisfied. I'm able to see you later today."

Take action: Set the appointment. Ask the owner to set aside a few hours to review the business and discuss the needs and desires you both have. Ask the owner to have the financial information, equipment lists, lease, and other documents on hand, so you both can use the time productively.

3

Pricing A Business

There are only three reasons a business won't sell:

The owner doesn't want to sell—in other words, is not motivated.

The owner wants an unreasonable price or unrealistic terms.

The "informed buyer" didn't educate the seller as to the terms and conditions necessary to make that business sell.

Important Points to Remember

There is no magic formula for estimating the equitable "selling price" of a business. Some people think that "rules of thumb," such as multiples (two times earnings, or some similar formula), are the way to price a business. But rules of thumb are rough guides at best. Whatever the selling price may be, however, you must work within some definite guidelines to make the selling price equitable for both buyer and seller:

Businesses selling for all cash usually won't sell.

People live out of their business. Calculating the seller's discretionary cash will give you the information necessary to establish the business's salabililty.

A fair down payment, terms and conditions, and market-rate interest are what make a deal work.

The Three Basic Elements

The basic elements in evaluating the price of a business are:

Fixtures and equipment: They can be market value, replacement value, or any other reasonable value the owner places on them. (If cost or replacement value is used, then deduct depreciation according to the age.)

Inventory or merchandise for resale: The inventory value is at the seller's cost.

Goodwill: This value depends on many factors, each of which must be considered when trying to establish the business's total value.

Seller's Discretionary Cash

Before we go any further, we must consider that people who are business owners live out of their business. One of the benefits of independent business ownership is the opportunity to collect "paid for" benefits, called perquisites (perks).

The seller's discretionary cash (SDC), then, is the total of the net profits of the business plus the salaries paid to owners and family members plus the value of the perks that are discretionary expenses.

The seller's discretionary expenses are determined by analyzing, with the seller, the seller's financial statements and all supporting documents, such as receipts and bills.

Review the following expenses carefully to determine the "paid for" benefits to the owner:

Rent
Supplies
Telephone
Utilities
Car expenses
Travel
Legal and accounting services
Interest on debt
Postage
Consultants
Salaries
Contract labor
Insurance

Advertising
Repairs
Maintenance
Payroll taxes
Personal property taxes
Laundry
Miscellaneous

Sales tax and city/state license fees are also discretionary cash items. In fact, any nonrecurring expense is a discretionary cash item.

Use the SDC from the business's last fiscal year. In the case of a rapidly growing business, use the net profit figure for the last six months and double it to arrive at an annual figure (but consider season variations).

Value of Fixtures/Equipment and Inventory

The money tied up in the fixtures and equipment (F&E) and inventory in a business purchase have an impact on the value of the business's goodwill.

Say that you are considering the purchase of one of the following businesses, both with the same SDC: (1) a service business requiring a minimum investment in F&E and inventory and (2) a manufacturing business requiring a significant investment in F&E and inventory. If you buy the manufacturing business, you will be required to tie up money that would otherwise be invested and earning a return (8 percent to 10 percent would be considered a reasonable return).

Because it takes more "tied up" money for the manufacturing business to realize the same SDC, then it is reasonable to make a downward adjustment of the goodwill value of the business. But devalue goodwill only if the value of F&E and inventory equals or exceeds $50,000, and then devalue it by only 10 percent of the value of the F&E and inventory.

Value of the Owner's or Manager's Services

The money paid for the owner's or manager's services also has an impact on the value of the business's goodwill.

The true net of the business is the amount of money left over for an owner after all actual and reasonable expenses are deducted. One of those expenses is the salary paid for the business's manager, which should be comparable to the prevailing salaries in the local job market.

Do not deduct the amount the owner actually takes out of the business. He or she may be taking a small amount for "walking-around" money or taking all the profits of the business.

In determining the worth of the owner's services, figure what it would take to replace the owner. For example, a person who owns and operates a card store grossing less than $250,000 could probably hire someone as a replacement for $12,000 to $16,000 a year. But a person operating a manufacturing plant employing fifty people and grossing $600,000 to $1 million a year might require $50,000 to $75,000 a year to replace the owner.

The salary expense for an owner's or manager's services is a judgment factor and should be carefully considered when assigning a value. The owner will be able to help you determine what it would cost to hire a manager to run the business. Deducting the value of the owner's or manager's services from the subtotal gives the true net generated by the business.

The Goodwill Multiplier

The goodwill might be valued at one to six times the true net of the business. Consider the following when trying to determine what multiplier to use:

> Most businesses should have a multiplier of 2.5 to 4. An attractive, rapidly growing business might have a multiplier of 3 to 4.5.
>
> Hard-to-sell businesses, where income depends on continual selling, may only have a multiplier of 1.

A 1.5, 2.5, or 3.5 multiplier would be used for a business that is above one multiplier but not quite to the next one. A Hallmark store may only be 2.5 if located in a poor location; an attractive health spa in a good location could be a 3.5.

If you are unsure of which multiplier to use, do an evaluation using two multipliers that seem appropriate to get a range to work from. Then negotiate with the owner to get the price.

Use the following information to arrive at the correct goodwill multiplier:

Venture rating (0 - 6):
  0 = Continuity of income at risk
  3 = Steady income likely
  6 = Growing income assured
Competitor rating (0 - 6):
  0 = Highly competitive (unstable) market
  3 = Normal competition
  6 = Little or no competition
Industry rating (0 - 6):
  0 = Declining growth rate
  3 = Growth faster than inflation
  6 = Outstanding growth
Business rating (0 - 6):
  0 = New business with no track record
  3 = Well-established business
  6 = Long-standing business with reputation
Growth rating (0 - 6):
  0 = Declining business
  3 = Growth faster than inflation
  6 = Outstanding growth record
Desirability rating (0 - 6):
  0 = No standing (undesirable)
  3 = Well-established business in good area
  6 = Outstanding business in upscale area

Rate the business in each of the six categories, from 1 to 6 (use 1.5, 2.5, 3.5, and so on to express slightly higher or lower ratings). Add up all the ratings and divide by 6 to arrive at your goodwill multiplier.

Experience, which you will gain from this book and from comparing the selling price of similar businesses that have been sold, will give you a better feel as to which multiplier you should use. Here are some other concerns:

Formula for Calculating Goodwill

Goodwill is a measure of a business's ability to make money. It is what remains after deducting from the seller's discretionary cash the worth of the owner's or manager's salary or services and 10 percent of the value of the fixtures, equipment, and inventory:

Seller's discretionary cash (SDC)		$ _____
10% of value of F&E and inventory (if over $50,000)		- _____
	Subtotal	$ _____
Value of owner's services		- _____
	True net of business	$ _____
Goodwill multiplier (between 1 and 6)		x _____
	GOODWILL VALUE	$ _____

Evaluating a Corporation Stock Sale

If you are buying the stock of a corporation, you must consider additional factors in evaluating the business. When you buy a corporation's stock, you are buying everything: cash in the bank, accounts payable, accounts receivable, taxes payable, fixtures and equipment, inventory, goodwill, and insurance policies.

Examine the balance sheets carefully. If the receivables are greater than the payables, it would be reasonable to add the difference to the selling price. But if the receivables are less than the payables, it would be reasonable to subtract the difference from the selling price.

Basically, valuing a corporation (stock sale) is the same as valuing any other company or business (asset sale). Add up all the assets, including the goodwill, and subtract all the liabilities to arrive at your selling price.

Things Never to Do and Things to Do

Some sellers will want to use a projected net income to help establish the business's selling price. Never do it! The business may not make the projected net income, in which case you will have paid too much for the business. If the net income does increase, it will be through your efforts and not the seller's.

Some sellers may want to charge for the lease value, often called leasehold interest rights. Never do it! You have already taken the lease value into acount when you calculated goodwill. If the rent had been higher, the net would have been lower and the goodwill less.

Many times you will come across a business that has no net profit. Don't think the business has no goodwill. The F&E's are installed, the doors are open, and the business has customers. A small business can be assigned $5,000 to $10,000 in goodwill, a larger one proportionately more. However, don't overdo it!

Often, more than one family member works in the business. Evaluate the owner's services based on the number of people that you, the new owner, need to replace. Also pay strict attention to who these people are, their specific duties, and the effect of their personality, longevity, and contacts on the business's income. This is a very important point.

Remember, the value of a business is sum of F&E, inventory, and goodwill. Do add the value of a special license, franchise fee, or whatever else has real tangible value. Don't add such items as commissions, value for lease, or anything else that doesn't have real, tangible value.

When a Business Is Priced Properly

A business that is priced properly is one where
The buyer will be able to operate the business.
The buyer will get a good return on the down payment.
The buyer will get paid for his or her services.
The buyer will be able to carry the debt service.
The buyer will make a nice profit.
Don't forget that you are the buyer.

Let's consider buying a business, a good business, in a wonderful location. (If any axiom still stands today it is "location, location, location.") The owner works the business full-time. These are the particulars:

SDC	$60,000
Inventory	$60,000
F&E	$40,000
Owner's services	$24,000

This is how we would establish the value for goodwill:

SDC	$60,000
Minus 10% of value of F&E and inventory	- 10,000
Subtotal	$50,000
Value of owner's services	- 24,000
True net of business	$26,000
Goodwill multiplier	x 3.0
GOODWILL VALUE	$78,000

The multiplier of 3 is appropriate because this is an attractive business with a good net profit.

To determine a fair selling price, we add the value of the F&E and inventory ($40,000 + $60,000) to the goodwill value ($78,000). By this calculation, the selling price of the business would be $178,000.

Is this a valid price? With a 39 percent downpayment of $53,400, we would have to get a return of $5,340 (10 percent) per year on the investment. The debt service on the remaining $126,000 for eight years at an interest rate of 10 percent is $1,890.70 per month, or $22,688.52 per year. With the salary ($24,000), we would have the following:

Return on investment	$ 5,340.00
Debt service	22,688.52
Salary for owner	24,000.00
TOTAL	$52,028.52

Deducting this total from our annual net of $84,000.00 (SDC plus owner's services), the business would show a very nice net profit of $31,971.48 annually. And we didn't even take into consideration owner's perks (the owner's discretionary expenses).

In other words, if you bought this business and all conditions remained the same, you could expect to recoup your investment in less than two years, your annual personal income would be in excess of $84,000, and you would have a solid business base for many years to come.

What is good about this arrangement is that both you and the seller are winners. You get a good solid business. The seller knows that he or she has sold the business to a person who will be responsible for it and also know that he or she will be assured of an annual income for eight years.

As you can see, the proper terms and interest are what make a deal work.

Guideline for Buying on Terms

With a few exceptions, businesses should be bought on terms. An exception would be a business making money that is priced at $25,000 or less. Here are some additional guidelines:

> Businesses priced reasonably with 30 percent or less down, are salable.

> The down payment should be equal to or less than one year's SDC.

> The seller should carry a note, secured by the business, for a term of three years or more depending on the premises' lease.

> The interest rate should be below prime.

> Let's say that the selling price of a business is $100,000 and the down payment is $30,000. The balance due the seller is then $70,000. That $70,000, fully amortized for five years, including 10 percent interest, is $1,487.30 per month.

If the profits of a business can't give a 10 percent return on your down payment, service the debt, pay an owner's or manager's salary, and still leave a profit, then you need to reevaluate the business's price or terms.

Remember, businesses are either difficult or impossible to sell if they are overpriced, if the down payment is too high, or the terms are unreasonable. The sellers who insist on all cash for their business are unrealistic. If they insist on all cash, inform them that in all likelihood the price will have to be discounted significantly. Then, as the prospective buyer, exercise the proper diligence to "prove out" the business.

Business Pricing Guidelines

Here are the most important points to remember:

Most businesses selling for all cash won't sell.

People live out of their business.

Calculating SDC will give you the true financials.

Terms and interest make the deal.

Here's the rule of thumb to use in determining the seller's true net profit:

Annual gross sales - Cost of goods sold - Fixed expenses = True net profit

Factors to Consider in Evaluating Price, Terms, and Value of Goodwill

Rent (what is fair?)

Lease, or economic rent factor (ERF)

Location (location, location, location)

Time established

Name and goodwill

Eye appeal

Sales history

Gross sales

Demand

Hours and days open

Sales of comparable businesses

Growth rates in area

Guidelines for Specific Types of Businesses

The following pricing guides will give you vital information to help determine the salability of certain types of businesses:

Bars/Taverns

Beer, wine, and liquor sales

Price should be 4 to 8 times monthly gross sales plus inventory.

Consider:

Who holds license and what license requirements are

Sales volume

What is owned by licensee and what is owned by vendors

Cocktail lounges

The license is more valuable than the license for bars and taverns because of the greater profit margin on alcoholic beverages sold by the drink. Price should be 5 to 10 times monthly gross sales.

Consider:

Who holds license and what license requirements are

Volume

What is owned by licensee and what is owned by vendors

Arrangement with live entertainment, if any

Liquor cost percentage

Cover charge

Fast Food

Independent operations

Price should be 4 to 6 times monthly gross sales plus inventory.

Consider:

Gross volume

Percentage of food and paper products cost

Ownership of vending machines

Franchised operations

Price (5 to 10 times monthly gross sales) generally includes franchise fee, monthly gross sales are usually higher than those of independents, demand is greater.

Consider:

Terms of franchise agreement
Franchise requirements for transfer
Percentage of royalty/transfer fee (who pays?).
Common advertising that may be the franchisee's obligation
Training school (how long and who pays?)
Territorial rights

Restaurants

No liquor

Price should be 4 to 6 times monthly gross sales plus inventory.

Consider:

Gross volume
Percentage of food costs
Labor costs
Chef's willingness to stay (if specialty restaurant)

Liquor

Liquor profits are double those of food, in most cases. Percentage of bar to food sales is determining factor. Greater the percentage of bar sales, higher the value. Price should be 5 to 10 times monthly gross sales.

Consider:

Ownership of license
Volume (food and liquor)
Equipment owned by vendors versus owner
Percentage of food versus liquor sales
Live entertainment costs (if any)
Chef's willingness to stay (if specialty restaurant)

Twenty-four-hour restaurant

Labor costs are higher because of hours and lower demand.

Price should be 3 to 6 times monthly gross sales.

Consider:

Gross volume
Percentage of food costs

Miscellneous Food Operations

Ethnic, specialty, or other restaurant

Price should be 4 to 7 times monthly gross sales plus inventory.

Consider:

    Franchise agreement (if applicable)

    Percentage of food costs

    Kind of specialty and demand in area

Cleaning Operations

Coin laundry

Age of equipment, rent, and gross sales are key factors in applying gross multiplier. Price should be 12 to 18 times monthly gross sales plus inventory.

Consider:

    Number of washers, dryers, and dry-cleaning machines

    Inclusion of wash-and-fold services or dry-cleaning pickup

    Presence of heat savers and dryers

    Time of wash cycle

    Charge to wash and dry per pound

    Age and brand of equipment

    Cost of utilities

Dry cleaner (plant or drop shop)

Price should be up to one year's net profit plus inventory and equipment

Consider:

    Gross volume

    Standard markup

    Capacity to do alterations

    Multiple locations

    Age, brand, and number of machines

    Franchise fees, if any

Markets

Market

Price should be 1 to 2 times monthly gross sales plus inventory

Consider:

    Gasoline allocation

    Percentage of food, gas, and liquor sales

    Ownership of licenses (gas, liquor, and so on) and license requirements

    Equipment under lease

Package/Liquor Stores

Package/liquor store

Value of liquor license is critical factor. Price should be 2 to 5 times monthly gross sales plus inventory.

Consider:
- Discounts on liquor
- Competition
- Gross volume of liquor versus beer and wine
- Ownership of license and requirements to have it
- Percentage of sales volume in smaller containers (half pints)
- Check-cashing services

Service Business

Sevice businesses in general

Price should be 1 year's net profit plus inventory plus equipment.

Consider:
- Skill, permit, or license required to deliver service
- Willingness of skilled employees or operators to stay

Tax service and bookkeeping

Price should be 1 year's gross sales plus all equipment

Consider:
- Gross volume of tax service versus bookkeeping service
- Requirement for CPA certification

Travel Agency

Most agencies average a slim 6 to 8 percent gross profit.

Price should be 8 to 10 percent of yearly gross sales for an established, fully appointed agency.

Consider:
- Number and type of established accounts
- Regulations required to be met
- Training required

Retail

Retail store

Price should be up to 1 year's net profit plus fixtures/ equipment and inventory.

Consider:
    Markup
    Wholesalers and distributors
    Seasonality of sales
    Inventory aging

Franchise Sales

New franchise

Price is established by franchisor; there is also a franchise fee. Existing franchises generally fall under one of the previous categories. Keep in mind that most franchise operations are in great demand and are profitable.

Miscellaneous

Wholesale or manufacturing firm

Price should be 1 to 2 year's net profit plus equipment plus inventory.

Consider:
    Wholesale markup
    Number of outside salespeople
    Costs of operation
    Relationships with labor unions

Terms

With few exceptions, you shouldn't buy a business for all cash. One exception is a business priced under $25,000. Businesses priced according to aforementioned guidelines are salable with 30 to 40 percent or less down. The down payment should be equal to or less than one year's net profit.

The seller should carry a note, secured by the business, for a term of three years or more, depending on the premises lease and the profits of the business. The interest rate should be below prime or, at best, the "going rate for the area."

Consider this example:

Selling price	$ 100,000
Down payment	35,000
Balance due seller	$ 65,000

The balance of $65,000 fully amortized for six years including 10 percent interest is $1,204.18 per month. If the profits of the business can't support your living wage and pay the debt, then you need to extend the period of the note or reduce the interest or both.

DISCRETIONARY CASH

The following are possible discretionary money sources for buyers on the seller's P & L statement.

Sales tax

Rent

Supplies

Telephone

Utilities

Car expenses

Travel

Legal

Accounting

Interest

Postage

Salaries

Contract labor

City/state license(s)

Insurance

Advertising

Repairs

Maintenance

Payroll taxes

Personal property taxes

Laundry

* Remember people live out of their businesses
* Any nonrecurring expense is a discretionary cash item

TERMS SUMMARY

Remember, the terms and interest make the deal work. You're looking for a low down payment, low monthly payments, and minimal balloon payments if required. Sellers want the current interest. The lower the entry fee and the lower the monthly payments, the better the chance for a safe, quick business sale.

4

Setting Up the Deal

You are going to face many interesting challenges in buying a business. How well these challenges are met will be a direct measure of your expertise and, ultimately, your success.

The first challenge actually is the first meeting with the business owner. During this meeting, the business owner will decide whether or not to do business with you. Remember that you can never make a good first impression the second time.

It is your responsibility to take charge of the interview by asking pertinent questions and, most of all, by listening carefully. Good business deals fail because of a failure to listen. If the business owner feels that you are interested in his or her situation and are concerned with his or her welfare, then the battle is half won.

Start by gathering all of the business's pertinent financial information. Find out the seller's goals and objectives for the future. This information is invaluable in determining not only what has motivated the decision to sell but also how to structure the sale in both parties' interests.

Don't volunteer a buying price or even ask what the seller wants before you thoroughly understand all facets of the business. A hastily contrived wrong answer may become embedded in the owner's mind and leave him or her feeling that the business is worth more than you discover it really is.

It is extremely important to thoroughly and accurately understand the business you are seeking to buy. Surprises will kill the sale and probably damage a second opportunity to buy it.

Know the market area where the business is located. Different businesses have different values, depending on where they are located. For example, a downtown business will sell for more or less than a like business in the suburbs.

Your ultimate goal is to

> Find a motivated seller.
> Know why the motivation exists.
> Work on buying a business that is priced right.
> Get all supporting materials and documentation to "prove out"
> the business.
> Negotiate terms and conditions that make sense.

This is hard, time-consuming work. It is also interesting, challenging, and rewarding once you buy the business that you have always been seeking to own.

Gathering of Pertinent Information

Be on time for your appointment with the seller, and allow at least two to three hours to gather the information on the business. Be accurate, and be complete. Do not discuss price early on. You will want to obtain all the pertinent information before you make a judgment about price.

Ask these questions of the owner, and record all data:

Business name: When the business is a sole proprietorship or partnership, record the trade name. When it is a corporation, use the trade name plus the designation Inc.

Address: Street, city, state, ZIP code.

Seller: If the business is a sole proprietorship, record the owner's name; if a partnership, record all partners' names and titles; if a corporation, record the names of all officers and their titles.

Business phone: Area code and number.

Building size: In square feet, from plans if possible.

Business description: Be specific and elaborate.

Allocated Assets: Record all assets that will remain with the business after the sale (tangible, or "hard," assets).

Inventory: Record all inventory that will transfer after the sale at the seller's cost.

Equipment and Fixtures: Enter the fair market value only.

Leasehold Improvements: Enter the market value of permanent improvements made by the seller to be transferred to the buyer after the sale.

Covenant not to compete: Amount of time the seller will promise not to compete in a "like" business and the designated number of miles from the business sold to the buyer.

Business trade name: Note whether it becomes part of the deal.

Licenses: Record what licenses are required and their cost annually or monthly.

Real property: If the business is sold with property, record a legal description and market value. You may require the service's of a real estate appraiser for this information.

Financial data: Obtain profit and loss statements for the past three years. Also get the latest quarterly statement so as to bring the business up to date.

Sales breakdown: Note sales or revenues over a certain period for the various product types or services the business offers. Break down the total sales by percentages to thoroughly understand how and why the business exists and where the sales are derived from.

Income and Expenses: Complete the following form accurately so as to determine the true net profit of the business.

Income
Gross sales $ _____
Cost of goods   _____

Gross profit $ _____

Expenses
    Rent $ _____
    Utilities _____
    Telephone _____
    Advertising _____
    Insurance _____
    Employee salaries _____
    Contract labor _____
    Auto/truck expense _____
    Accounting/legal services _____
    Maintenance _____
    Repairs _____
    Depreciation or replacement fund _____
    Taxes _____
    Equipment rental _____
    Equipment lease _____
    Supplies _____
    Owner's salary _____
    Miscellaneous _____
                       Total expenses $ _____

Net operating profit before income tax $ _____
    (gross profit less total expenses) $ _____

When dealing with P&L statements, you must scrutinize the expenses to determine the amount of "fringe benefits" involved. If you do not spend money on these fringe benefits, the available dollars will be added to net operating profit and become taxable.

Total net: Enter the sum of the seller's draw, business net income, fringe benefits, and depreciation.

Existing business encumbrances: Record the total debt against the business, to whom it is owed, the amount remaining, interest rate, and monthly payments. If there is no debt, then the business will be free and clear at close of escrow.

Existing real property encumbrances: Same as above if real property is included in the sale.

Lease information: Name and address of lessor.

Zoning: Determine the exact use of the property from the zoning board.

Lease information: Determine the exact month and year that the lease expires and the number and terms of options for renewal.

Security deposits: Are there any, and how much are they?

Additional lease charges: Proportionate portion of real estate taxes, trash removal, percentage of income, and so on.

Age of business and length of time owned by seller: Two questions, answered in months and years.

Incorporation: If the business is incorporated, determine the state and the year of incorporation.

Number of employees: Full-time, part-time, and owners.

Product(s): Type and method of distribution.

Accounting: Month that year ends.

Hours: Days and hours that business is open.

Seller's reason for selling: Very important. Also ask the seller what he or she is going to do after the sale. Spend some time here to really get to know the seller's motivations.

Training: Will the seller train the buyer? If yes, for how long?

Equipment for sale: Make a list.

Equipment under rental or lease: Make a list.

Books and records of the business: Will they verify sales and profits? If they do, you are in good shape. If they don't, how can the "true net" be proven by the seller?

Inventory: How much will be transferred with the business at the seller's cost? Is the inventory included in the total price?

Equipment: What is the approximate replacement value of all equipment included in the assets for sale (in present condition)?

Legal action: Is there any pending against the business?

Never predict or talk about the future, and avoid the word potential. Always keep your conversation centered around what the business has done and what it is presently doing.

The following worksheets will be invaluable as you get into the heart of the business you want to buy. Record all data of the business on the following worksheets. Be exact, be accurate, do not guess or project into the future, and above all be totally realistic. This is not the time to "fall in love" with the business. Reserve that wonderful emotion after the business proves to be what the seller has been telling you all along. There is also a form to get your own financials in order to see if you have the financial means to purchase the business of your dreams.

Corporate Resolution

If the business you are seeking to buy is a corporation, then it will be necessary for you to have a corporate resolution. This document enables you to know that the corporation has authorized a specific board member as its representative in the transaction of sale.

The sale or transfer of stock as a method of selling a corporation is complex. As the buyer, you will be assuming any liabilities, and you are subject to complex tax laws. You must use due diligence to prove that the business is what it was purported to be. A broker, a lawyer, or your accountant can verify the information and the financials for you if you choose. From a realistic point of view, and in the final analysis, you will assume all of the responsibilities. That is why I stress your complete involvement in the buying process. You should gather the information and then use an accountant to verify the financials of the company you have totally reviewed. Hire an attorney to put on paper the essence of the contractual deal that you and the seller have hammered out to your mutual benefit. Remember this: If both buyer and seller don't get a good deal—a win-win situation or as close to a 50/50 deal as possible—there won't be a sale.

If you found the business through a business broker, allow the broker to gather information for you. But remember this: The broker was hired by the seller (in most cases) and will collect a commission from the seller only after the business sells. Be careful, be exacting, and be totally informed about the business you are going to buy.

Corporate Resolution

I, _____, Secretary of _____, a _____ Corporation, do hereby certify that the following is a true and correct copy of the resolution unanimously adopted by the Board of Directors of the said Corporation, a quorum of its members being present at the regular business meeting, held in the city of _____, County, _____ on the ____ day of _____ 19___, and that this resolution has not been revoked by any subsequent action of the Board of Directors of said Corporation but is still in full force and effect.

> "Be it resolved, that _____, the _____ of the said Corporation, is hereby authorized and directed, with full and complete authority, to perform any necessary act to grant to _____ the authorization to sell, lease, or exchange certain assets of said Corporation."

_____
Secretary of Corporation

STATE OF _____

SS

COUNTY OF _____

On the ____ day of _____, 19___, before me, the under-signed Notary Public, personally appeared   , known personally to me to be the Secretary of   , an   Corporation, and he/she as such officer, being authorized so to do, executed the foregoing instrument for the sole purpose contained therein, by signing the name of the Corporation by himself/herself as said Secretary. IN WITNESS WHEREOF, I have hereunto set my hand and official seal.

_____
Notary Public

(Notarial Seal)   My Commission Expires _____, 19____

Business Expense Worksheet

This worksheet is used to separate the expenses necessary for business operation from those expenses that primarily benefit the business owner. Remember, most business owners live out of their business. If you are to properly view the business as the buyer, then you must know for what purposes the dollars are being spent.

Business Expense Worksheet

Business name _____ Date _____

Expenses are from _____ Tax statment _____ P&L _____Estimated

Fiscal year ends _____, 19 _____

Fixed Expenses	Variable Expenses	Perks
Rent........................ _____	Owner's draw............. _____	_____
Business telephone. _____	Payroll........................ _____	_____
Business utilities .... _____	Payroll taxes............... _____	_____
Real estate taxes ..... _____	Personal insurance ..... _____	_____
Licenses.................. _____	Repairs .... _____	_____
Water/sewer .... _____	Supplies...................... _____	_____
Franchise fee .... _____	Legal/accounting........ _____	_____
Business auto .... _____	Advertising.................. _____	_____
Equipment rental.... _____	Entertainment............. _____	_____
Equipment lease ..... _____	Personal auto.............. _____	_____
Other...................... _____	Travel .... _____	_____
Other...................... _____	Interest....................... _____	_____
Other...................... _____	Other.......................... _____	_____
Total Fixed Expenses................. _____	Total Variable Expenses..................... _____	_____

Noncash Expense
   Depreciation............ _____
   Amortization.............. _____

Total Expense............ _____
Seller's Discretionary
Expenses.................... _____

Miscellaneous comments _____

_____

_____

Fixed expenses are those necessary for the operation of the business only. Gather information on each expense and determine if they will remain the same or change after the sale (for instance, will there be an increase in rent?). If there will be a change, note it in the comments section and later compute future business expenses as they will affect your sales (and income).

The variable expenses vary depending on certain needs of the business or depending on the goals the owner is trying to achieve. Examples would be intensive advertising or hiring additional employees for a special campaign. Stashed away in the variable expenses are certain of the owner's benefits. Find out what they are and how much they are worth in gross dollars.

Perquisites, or perks, are the benefits that a business owner derives from the business above and beyond the salary or dividend compensation. Again, thoroughly examine each expense carefully to derive, with the owner's help, his or her personal benefit.

Review the financials for depreciation and amortization, which are *noncash expense*. These are allowable paper deductions that translate into dollars because they go directly to the bottom line in the form of profits to the business owner.

The seller's discretionary expenses are all of the dollars spent that are not necessary for the operation of the business. These dollars become available to a new owner as part of the buyer's discretionary cash.

Business Analysis Worksheets

Use these forms to determine the available cash flow and other important data that will help you decide whether to buy the business.

Business Analysis Worksheet: Pro Forma Cash Flow

Business name _____ Date _____

Estimated sales $ _____

Estimated cost of goods $ _____

Estimated gross profit............................$ _____

Estimated Expenses

Fixed Expenses		Variable Expenses	
Rent.......................	_____	Payroll.......................	_____
Business telephone.	_____	Payroll taxes...............	_____
Business utilities	_____	Repairs	_____
Real estate taxes	_____	Supplies.......................	_____
Licenses.................	_____	Advertising.................	_____
Water/sewer	_____	Legal/accounting........	_____
Franchise fee	_____	Other............................	_____
Business auto	_____	Other............................	_____
Equipment rental....	_____	Other............................	_____
Equipment lease	_____	Other............................	_____
Other......................	_____	Other............................	_____
Other......................	_____	Other.	_____
Total Fixed Expenses................	_____	Total Variable Expenses....................	_____

Total Estimated Expense............................ _____

Estimated Debt Service.............................. _____

Estimated Cash Flow................................ _____

Notes _____

_____

_____

Business Analysis Worksheet: Business Data

Business name _____ Date _____

GENERAL: Established 19___ Employees ___ FT ___ PT ___ Owners

Days open _____ Closed on _____ Hours _____

Revenue breakdown: _____ - _____, _____ - _____, _____ - _____,

_____ - _____, _____ - _____, _____ - _____, _____ - _____,

PREMISE LEASE INFORMATION: Building size   sq.ft. Parking

Base rent/month $_____ Security $_____ Option(s) _____

Lease expiration date _____ Lease/terms & conditions _____

Miscellaneous lease information_____

_____

INCLUDED WITH BUSINESS:

Furniture & equipment $ _____ Other $ _____

Including all trade fixtures and

equipment except _____ Describe_____

_____

Inventory at cost $_____ Seller will train for _____ weeks

BUSINESS ASKING PRICE AND TERMS: _____

		Real estate _____	With business
		_____	Optional

Price	$_____	Price	$_____
Down payment	$_____	Down payment	$_____

Balance $_____ at $____/month Balance $_____ at $____/month

(___ months) incl. ___% interest/yr. (___ months) incl. ___% interest/yr.

Additional terms _____ Additional terms_____

_____   _____

_____   _____

Reason for sale_____

Notes _____

_____

Business Pricing Worksheet

This worksheet can be used to establish a business's value and terms or to evaluate the seller's estimate. The data derived from this worksheet will only be valuable if the information is accurate.

Business Pricing Worksheet

Business name _____ Date _____

Figures from ___Tax statement ___P&L ___Estimated ___Year

1. Hard assets
   a. Fixtures & equipment..... _____
   b. Inventory......................... _____
   c. Other (_____) .... _____ $_____

2. Net profit (loss) $_____

3. Owner(s) salary, if included in business expenses   _____

4. Seller's discretionary expenses
   (from Business Expense Worksheet)   _____

5. Nonrecurring expenses (from Business Expense Worksheet)   _____

6. Noncash expense (from Business Expense Worksheet)
   a. Depreciation   _____
   b. Amortization   _____

7. Real estate expense (if owned)
   a. Property taxes   _____
      Repairs   _____
      Other   _____
   b. Rent (subtract)   (_____) _____

8. Seller's discretionary
   cash (lines 2-7) $_____

9. Adjustments (subtract from line 8)
   a. 10% of fixtures/equipment
      and inventory if selling price
      is over $50,000   _____
   b. Owner's services   _____ (_____)

10. True net of business
    (line 8 minus line 9) $_____

11. Goodwill (multiply true net
    by goodwill multiplier given
    to the business)   x_____$_____

12. Recommended business selling price
    (line 1 plus line 11) $_____
                                                        ....

13. Real estate value (from real estate
    value worksheet—subordinate ___yes ___no $_____

14. Total value of business and real estate
    (line 12 plus line 13) $_____
                                                        ....

15. Recommended terms:
    Down payment (30% of line 14) $_____
    Debt service (25% of line 8) $_____ per year

16. Seller's terms:
    Down payment $_____
    Debt service $_____ per year

17. Analysis:
    Seller's discretional cash (line 8) $_____
    minus Return on investment
         (10% of down payment) $_____
    minus Debt service $_____
    minus Owner's services $_____ =$_____
                                                        Profit or loss

Notes: _____
_____
_____
_____
_____

The price derived through the Business Pricing Worksheet takes into consideration a selling price that is low because of a short-term lease or because the business requires initially long hours of operation by a new owner. Use your judgment when determining what multiplier to use in determining the business's selling price.

Real Estate Value Worksheet

If real estate is involved in the business sale, either as an option or as part of the selling price, you must commmplete the Real Estate Value Worksheet to determine the combined business and real estate selling price. Review with the seller the impact that the real estate value will have on your incremental cash requirements and that the debt service will have on you and your discretionary cash flow.

Real Estate Value Worksheet

Business name _____ Date _____

Figures from ___Tax statement ___P&L ___Estimated ___Year

Real estate value—Income Approach

1. Gross income
    (rental income   actual   estimate) $_____

2. Expenses
    a. Property taxes................. _____
    b. Repairs........................... _____
    c. Other(s).......................... _____

3. Net income (line 1 minus line 2)   _____

4. Capitalization rate................. ___/___.__

5. Real estate value
    (income approach)................ _____

Real Estate Debt Service

6. Real estate value
    ___Income approach
    ___Seller wants
    ___Appraisal..................... $_____

7. Down payment..................... _____

8. Return on down payment (multiply
    line 7 by 10% return)........................... $_____

9. Balance financed
    (line 6 minus line 7).............. _____

10. Monthly payments
    (___months at ___%)........... _____

11. Yearly payments (multiply line 10
    by 12 payments)................................... $_____

12. Required cash flow to Service
    Real Estate (line 8 plus line 11) ....$_____

Review additional down payment and cash flow requirements

Will seller subordinate? ___yes ___no

This worksheet has two sections: valuing real estate from an income approach and calculating the real estate debt service.

In this method, the real estate is valued on its net income and the return on investment (ROI) required to make purchasing the real estate viable.

The capitalization rate has a significant impact on the recommended selling price. The capitalization rate is a rate of interest used to convert a series of future payments into a single present value. It is used to derive the capital value of an income stream. The formula:

$$\text{Value} = \frac{\text{Annual income}}{\text{Capitalization rate}}$$

For example if the estimated net operating income of a business is $60,000 and you determine a capitalization rate of 12 percent, then the estimated value of the real estate is $500,000.

To determine the real estate value, find the gross income and subtract the expenses to determine net income. Determine the capitalization rate and divide the net income by that rate. This will give you the real estate value based on its ability to earn money.

Real Estate Debt Service

Whether through an evaluation of the real estate by return on investment, appraisal, or seller's demand, you will arrive at a value. Use this value and the asking down payment and terms to calculate the real estate debt service. Also include a 10 percent cost-of-money value for the down payment to evaluate the required cash flow to service the real estate dabt.

Will the Seller Subordinate?

Determine if the seller is willing to take a secondary position to a lending institution on the real estate. This will give you an option for another source of money to buy the property rather than out of your pocket. If the seller is willing to subordinate, then the requirements for the down payment can be significantly reduced in a majority of cases.

Supplemental Information Worksheet

The information on this worksheet will enable you to better understand the business you would like to buy. Be as descriptive as possible to help yourself get a crystal-clear and accurate picture of all aspects of the business.

All sections of the form are self-explanatory except for Section 1 (Financial Data).

Supplemental Information

Business name _____ Date _____

1. Financial data:	Prior Year 19__	Last Year 19__	This Year 19__	Robert Morris Guideline
Sales	_____	_____	_____	_____
Cost of goods	_____	_____	_____	_____
Gross profit	_____	_____	_____	_____
Expenses	_____	_____	_____	_____
Net profit	_____	_____	_____	_____
Owner's salary	_____	_____	_____	_____
Inventory/ equipment	_____	_____	_____	_____
Net worth	_____	_____	_____	_____
Total	_____	_____	_____	_____

2. Description of business:
   History of business _____
   _____
   _____
   _____

   Type of services, product lines, accounts, etc. _____
   _____
   _____
   _____

   Competition _____
   _____
   _____
   _____

   Marketing strategies, advertising, etc. _____
   _____
   _____
   _____
   _____
   _____

3. Description of facilities: ___Owned ___Leased
   Condition of property (inside and out) _____
   _____
   _____
   _____

   Condition of general area and nearby businesses _____
   _____
   _____
   _____

4. General comments:
   Strengths _____

   _____

   _____

   _____

   Weaknesses_____

   _____

   _____

   _____

5. Additional information:
   Are outsiders aware that the business is for sale? ___yes ___no
   Are employees aware that the business is for sale? ___yes ___no
   Does the business make sense? ___yes ___no
   Why does/doesn't the business make sense? _____

   _____

   _____

   _____

   _____

   What is my "gut" feeling about the business?_____

   _____

   _____

   _____

   _____

This information is obtained from the seller's financial reports and tax records. You must determine if the information truly reflects the actual performance of the business. For example, if the sales figure is accurate, the cost of goods may be overinflated, or if the cost of goods is accurate, sales may be underinflated.

Evaluate the business according to the "rules" previously given to you. Specific evaluation guidelines can be obtained by visiting your local library's business section and looking at the latest copy of Robert Morris Associates' *Annual Statement Studies*. This information can be used to help you get a better feel for business's typical performance and what you might expect should you purchase that business.

It is virtually impossible to evaluate most businesses based solely on the tax statements or financial reports. You need to understand three things:

The underground economy does exist.

Business owners live out of their business.

Tax statements and financial reports benefit the seller and not the buyer.

Checklist

All data must be accurate and complete. Your goal is to cover all facets of the business being sold. A lazy or inadvertent mistake could cost you thousands of dollars, if not more. So do yourself a big favor: Don't be lazy any step of the way.

Checklist

Business name _____ Date _____

Key Items	Yes	No
Does the business make sense?..............................	____	____
Is the reason for the sale fully understood?...........	____	____
Are all data complete?...	____	____
Do I feel good about the business?........................	____	____
Are the numbers right?...	____	____
Has the lessor been contacted?.............................	____	____
Consent to assign?......................................	____	____
Consent for sublease?.................................	____	____
Consent for new lease?...............................	____	____
Terms acceptable?......................................	____	____
Are there any problems with the seller's		
Sales tax returns?......................................	____	____
IRS withholding?..	____	____
Mortgage payments?...................................	____	____
Financing statement or liens?.......................	____	____
Is the seller in compliance with		
Zoning laws?...	____	____
Health and safety laws?...............................	____	____
Fire and health requirements?.......................	____	____
Copy of last inspection?..............................	____	____

Backup Material

	Yes	No
Corporate resolution..	____	____
Equipment list...	____	____
Copy of lease...	____	____
Franchise Agreement..	____	____
Financials..	____	____
Three years..	____	____
Tax statements..	____	____
Three years..	____	____
Sales tax reports..	____	____
Three years..	____	____
Expense worksheet...	____	____
Pricing worksheet..	____	____
Real estate worksheet...	____	____

Supplemental information ____ ____

The price and terms should make sense, the documentation should be complete, the lessor (landlord) should be contacted and all obstacles removed, the equipment should be operational, and all indebtedness and compliances should be understood and under control.

Remember, surprises kill deals!

Buyer's Financial Worksheet

This worksheet will enable you to truly see yourself from an asset and liability standpoint. Be as accurate as possible, because you may have to present this form to a financial institution to obtain the funds to purchase your business. You are actually preparing a written record of your own financial status.

Buyer's Financial Worksheet
Statement Made as a Basis of Credit Giving
Financial Condition as of _____, 19__

CURRENT ASSETS	CURRENT LIABILITIES
Cash on hand in banks .... _____	(Due within 1 year ea. caption)
Accts receivable (what your customers owe you and not pledged or sold to others)...... _____	Accts. Payable — not due..... _____ Accts. Payable — past due.... _____ Notes Payable — Banks
Cash surrender value Life Insurance........................ _____	Monthly Payments ($).... _____ R.E. Mortgages— Mo.
Stocks & Bonds Salable Merch. at Cost (not on consignment or conditional sale).. _____	Home Payment ($) Other ($).... _____ Equip/Merch. Debt Secured by Mortgage
Other Current (Detail).......... _____	Mo. Payment ($).... _____
TOTAL CURRENT ASSETS ....$_____	Loans — Mo. ($).... _____ Per. Installment Debt............. _____ Other Debt (detail)................ _____ TOTAL LIABILITIES.......... _____

FIXED ASSETS
Business

R.E. (Current Value)........... _____

Equip. (Current Value)...... _____

Vehicles (Yr. & Model)... _____

Other Assets (Detail)....... _____

Personal

Home (Current Value) .... _____

Furniture (Value)............. _____

Vehicles (Yr. & Model)... _____

Other (Describe)................ _____

Total Fixed Assets............. _____

Total Assets .... _____

LONG TERM
LIABILITIES

R.E. Mortgages
Residence   ($)
Other   ($).... _____

Notes Payable — Banks........ _____

Equip/Merch. Debt
Secured by Mortgage............ _____

Other Long Term
Obligations (Detail).............. _____

Total Long Term Liab........... _____

Total Liabilities .... $_____

Net Worth (All Assets
Less Liabilities..................... $_____

TOTAL LIABILITIES &
NET WORTH.................... $_____

Operating Plan Forecast

Use this worksheet to plan and forecast the cash needs of the business you are buying for a period of one year from the date you become its owner. Use the hard data that has proven the business to be reliable. Do the forecast several different ways: "What if I worked an additional ten hours per week, how would that affect sales?" "What if I eliminated some costly overhead, like an extra employee or excessive advertising? How would that positively affect my bottom line?" Be creative, but don't expect to change things too much too soon. You could destroy a solid business that is making good profits. Changes can and should be made prudently over a period of time so as to assure a positive direction.

Operating Plan Forecast — P & L Projection

DATA	JANUARY EST.	JANUARY ACT.	JANUARY %	FEBRUARY EST.	FEBRUARY ACT.	FEBRUARY %	MARCH EST.	MARCH ACT.	MARCH %
Revenue (Sales)									
Total Revenue									
Cost of Sales									
Total C.O.S.									
Gross Profit									
Expenses									
Salaries									
Payroll Exp's									
Outside Serv.									
Supplies									
Repairs/Maint									
Advertising									
Auto Exp.									
Accounting									
Legal									
Rent									
Telephone									
Utilities									
Insurance									
Taxes									
Interest									
Depreciation									
Other Exps.									

68

Operating Plan Forecast — P & L Projection

DATA	APRIL EST.	ACT.	%	MAY EST.	ACT.	%	JUNE EST.	ACT.	%	JULY EST.	ACT.	%	AUGUST EST.	ACT.	%
Revenue (Sales)															
Total Revenue															
Cost of Sales															
Total C.O.S.															
Gross Profit															
Expenses															
Salaries															
Payroll Exp's															
Outside Serv.															
Supplies															
Repairs/Maint															
Advertising															
Auto Exp.															
Accounting															
Legal															
Rent															
Telephone															
Utilities															
Insurance															
Taxes															
Interest															
Depreciation															
Other Exps.															

Operating Plan Forecast — P & L Projection

DATA	Ind. %	SEPTEMBER EST.	ACT.	%	OCTOBER EST.	ACT.	%	NOVEMBER EST.	ACT.	%	DECEMBER EST.	ACT.	%
Revenue (Sales)													
Total Revenue													
Cost of Sales													
Total C.O.S.													
Gross Profit													
Expenses													
Salaries													
Payroll Exp's													
Outside Serv.													
Supplies													
Repairs/Maint.													
Advertising													
Auto Exp.													
Accounting													
Legal													
Rent													
Telephone													
Utilities													
Insurance													
Taxes													
Interest													
Depreciation													
Other Exps.													

5

Filling in the Blanks

In order to properly analyze the details of a business, you will need to know specifics. Through questions and answers, you can expand your knowledge of a business in order to make the decision whether to buy or "pass."

Often a seller will wonder why a buyer didn't call back. The reason in many cases is that the seller or broker is unprepared to properly and adequately present the business. Remember, as a buyer you will "buy" the seller before you will buy the business. If the seller or broker doesn't present business information in a knowledgeable and professional manner, then chances are you won't buy the business.

Being prepared and being able to properly understand a business requires that you have the right information at the right time. The right time is when you are comfortable with the seller and are receptive to his or her information.

Each type of business has certain crucial types of information specific to itself. Detail that information on your worksheets, and you will have a lot more confidence in your ability to get the job done.

The following information is what you must find out in addition to the normal business information required to complete your analysis. I have outlined many different types of businesses in different categories. I have done so to give you more to think about, so you are able to complete your business analysis. Regardless of the type of business you're interested in, scan them all. Use the thoughts and questions interchangeably from category to category and business to business, as long as they fit and make sense.

Taverns

- Beer or Beer and Wine Only
  - Holder of license
  - License requirements
  - Number and types of kegs sold
  - Types of bottled beer and wine sold
  - Revenue (tap/glass/bottle)
  - Costs (tap/glass/bottle)
  - Price (tap/glass/bottle)
  - Other revenue (electronic games, jukebox)
  - Tournaments
  - Owner of fixtures and equipment (licensee or vendors)
  - Type of food and sales

Cocktail Lounges

- All types of beverages
  - Holder of license
  - License requirements
  - Pour costs per drink
  - Happy hour prices
  - Number and types of kegs sold
  - Types of bottled beer and wine sold
  - Revenue (tap/glass/bottle/liquor)
  - Costs (tap/glass/bottle/liquor)
  - Price (tap/glass/bottle/liquor)

- Other revenue (electronic games, jukebox)
- Owner of fixtures and equiment (licensee or vendor)
- Type of food and sales
- Arrangements with live entertainment
- Cover charge

Fast Food Restaurants

- Franchised operations (usually higher monthly gross sales than independents and in greater demand)
  - Franchise agreement
  - Transfer provisions in franchise agreement and transfer fees
  - Royalty and common advertising fee to franchisor
  - Duration and cost of training school
  - Territorial rights
- Independent operations
  - Gross volume
  - Food and paper costs as percentage of sales
  - Owner of vending machines and electronic games

Restaurants

- Coffee shops
  - Meals served (breakfast, lunch, dinner)
  - Average number of meals served weekly
  - Average ticket value
  - Type of food served
  - Income from electronic games
  - Beer and wine license
  - Type of advertising
- Dinner restaurants with cocktails
  - Meals served (breakfast, lunch, dinner)
  - Number of meals served weekly
  - Food sales versus cocktail sales
  - Types and quantity of seating
  - Owner of liquor license
  - Owner of fixtures and euipment

- Cover charge
- Live entertainment costs
- Cook's plans to stay if a specialty restaurant
- Food, beer/wine, and alcoholic beverage costs
- Type of food served

Other Food Businesses

- Bakeries
  - Products baked
  - Revenue (retail versus wholesale)
  - Cost of goods (retail versus wholesale)
  - Cost of delivery service
  - Number of routes
  - Disposition of stale or day-old products
  - Compensation plan for drivers
  - Guaranteed sales at clients' stores

- Caterers
  - Types (wedding, business, private party, and so on)
  - Types of food offered
  - Number of bookings per month
  - Availability of banquet hall
  - Liquor license
  - Sandwich shops
  - Types of sandwiches
  - Average number of sandwiches sold per day
  - Food costs as percentage of sales
  - Sources of customers
  - Beer/wine or liquor license

Cleaning Operations

- Coin laundries
  - Number of washers, dryers, and dry-cleaning machines
  - Type of operation (wash and fold or dry-cleaning pickup station)
  - Heat savers on dryers
  - Time of wash cycle
  - Charge to wash and dry

- Charge per pound to wash and fold
- Age and brand of euqipment
- Cost of utilities

- Dry-cleaning plants
  - Age, brand, and number of machines
  - Size of boiler, sniffer, and filter(s)
  - Charge for dry cleaning (men's and women's prices per piece and clothing type)
  - Work in progress (work on racks)
  - Facilities for doing alterations
  - Delivery services
  - Revenue (contracts, wholesale, local)
  - Laundry services (shirts, wash and fold, and so on)
  - Gross volume, markup, alterations capability and locations of satellite "drop shops"

Markets

- Delicatessens
  - Amount of catering
  - Types and costs of food sold
  - Delivery services
  - Revenue (prepared food versus shelf items)
  - Owner of beer/wine or liquor license
  - Owner of fixtures and equipment

- Markets and convenience stores
  - Gasoline allocation
  - Charge accounts
  - Delivery service
  - Back room stock value
  - Wholesale sources
  - Franchise fees and costs
  - Percentages of food, gas, and beer/wine sales
  - Owner of beer/wine license
  - Requirements for beer/wine license
  - Owner of machinery and equipment

Package/Liquor Stores

- Package liquor stores
  - Discounts
  - Gross volume (beer/wine versus liquor)
  - Owner of license
  - Requirements for license
  - Revenue from sundries sold
  - Percentage of sales in smaller containers (half pints)

Service Businesses

- Service businesses in general
  - Skill, permit, or license required to deliver service
  - Plans of skilled employees or operators to stay

- Air-conditioning firms
  - Dollar amount of sales (repair versus service)
  - Sheet metal shop
  - Number of service accounts
  - Number of new-home installations

- Answering service
  - Number of established accounts
  - Number of telephone boards
  - Capacity of each board
  - Hours of service provided
  - Primary client type

- Auto body and paint shops
  - Percentage of insurance work
  - Number of work bays
  - OSHA compliance
  - Types of cars worked on (domestic, foreign, specialty)

- Auto repair shops
  - Number of work bays
  - Method of paying
  - Major accounts
  - Volume of specialty vehicle repair

- Machine shop
- Parts sales

- Auto washes
  - Price of wash
  - Number of washes per month
  - Type of equipment
  - Gross and net profits
  - Water recycling
  - Associated sales from gasoline, oil, and auto parts
  - Extra services, such as auto detail work

- Beauty/hair salons
  - Method of paying operaters (commission or salary)
  - Cost and markup of supplies
  - Involvement of owner (operator)
  - Owner's gross profit
  - Number of chairs
  - Manicures and associated services offered

- Card rooms
  - Number of tables
  - Dealers provided
  - Charges per hour
  - Income from food
  - Licensing of tables

- Dog/pet grooming services
  - Number of regular customers
  - Charges
  - Method of paying groomers
  - Pet products sold, markup, and profits

- Employment agency
  - Major accounts
  - Percentage fee charged per placement
  - Number of job listings
  - Specialties
  - Longevity and monthly billings of account executives

- Gardening/landscaping services
  - Number of accounts
  - Types of accounts (residential versus commercial)
  - Prices charged
  - Monthly gross profit versus cost of goods
  - Location of accounts

- Insurance agencies
  - Number of producers
  - Total premiums
  - Computerization
  - Number of policies and gross commissions
  - Commercial percentage
  - Personal percentage
  - Seller's plans to stay in the business
  - Number of employees
  - Number of carriers
  - Loss ratio
  - Brokerage amount
  - Condition of trust account
  - Largest account
  - Type of insurance carried

- Interior decorating services
  - Major activity in decorating
  - Source of supplies
  - Ratio of residential to commercial business
  - Seller's plans to stay in the business

- Janitorial services
  - Size and type of accounts
  - Monthly gross profits
  - Longevity and skills of janitors
  - Method of paying employees
  - Location of accounts

- Lock and safe services
  - Volume of sales
  - Volume of service

- Major accounts
- Mobile service provided
- Lines carried

- Machine shops
  - Number of accounts
  - Type of (production of job) shop
  - General type of work produced
  - Specialties and skilled labor required

- Mailing services
  - Types of services offered (printing, list selecting, label affixing, hand-addressing, inserting, collating, folding, sorting, selling postage, and so on)
  - Mailing list types (business, new business, residential, specialty)
  - Longevity and market share of business versus competition

- Photo studios
  - Types of camera equipment
  - Number and types of lighting
  - Outside services provided
  - Darkroom facilities (or outside laboratory)
  - Type of work

- Plating companies
  - Production or job shop
  - Types of plating
  - Cost of goods based on type (gold, silver, and so on)
  - Number and size of tanks
  - Number and types of polishing equipment

- Pool services
  - Number and location of accounts
  - Monthly gross profit
  - Charges
  - Supplies sold
  - Revenue from service versus repairs

- Preschool day-care facilities
  - Number of children licenses for

- Number of enrolled full and part-time
- Charges for full and part-time
- Room to expand
- Food service offered
- Who are the employees? Do they meet state qualifications?

- Print shops
  - Number of accounts
  - Types of printing services offered
  - Color capacity
  - Independent or franchise operation
  - Computerization
  - Type setting available
  - Binding facilities

- Real estate agencies
  - State requirements
  - Commission splits with salespeople
  - Gross commissions earned last year
  - Tone of market (residential and/or commercial)
  - Number of listings
  - Insurance needed

- Rental equipment services
  - Type of equipment rented
  - Age of equipment
  - Percentage of commercial versus private business
  - Owner of equipment

- Service stations
  - Cost of gasoline and related products
  - Profit margin per grade of gasoline
  - Percentage of revenues from repair work
  - Gallons pumped per month
  - Number of work bays
  - Gasoline storage capacity
  - Number of hoists
  - Number of islands and pumps
  - Availability of new franchise or same lease

- Length of lease
- Sales of food or snack shop in gross dollars per month and as percentage of gross and net profits

- Sign shops
  - Types of signs produced
  - Number of and income from leased signs

- Tax and bookkeeping services
  - Gross volume of tax versus bookkeeping service
  - Number of accounts
  - Number of tax accounts
  - Charge for bookkeeping and tax services
  - Computerization
  - Single-entry versus double-entry accounts
  - Frequency of statements
  - CPA certification requirement

- Towing services
  - Number of trucks
  - Contracts with local police
  - Storage capacity
  - Auto club contracts
  - Auto body shop contracts

- Travel agencies
  - Number and size of established accounts
  - Appointments held and manager's qualification for appointments
  - Competition
  - Income from ticket sales and tour sales
  - Percentage of commissions from commercial accounts
  - Regulations required to be met

- Trucking firms
  - Licenses and permits held
  - Area covered
  - Year and type of vehicles
  - PUC license

- Carpet and upholstery cleaners
  - Percentage of business accounts
  - Apartment complex contracts
  - Type of equipment
  - Insurance

Retail Businesses

- Retail businesses in general
  - Size of markup
  - Wholesalers and distributors serving business
  - Major brands carried
  - Seasonality of sales
  - Inventory aging
- Arts and crafts shops
  - Kinds of merchandise
  - Income from instruction
  - Specialty offerings
- Auto parts stores
  - Brands carried
  - Delivery services
  - Major accounts
  - Inventory control (computerization)
  - Availability of tires, brakes, and alignment
  - Equipment rental
  - Inventory turnover rate
  - Domestic or foreign inventory
- Auto dealers
  - New versus used cars
  - Pecentage of sales from repairs
  - Inventory of new and used cars
  - Source of used cars
  - Financing available for customers
  - Advertising
  - Floor costs
  - Other services

- Auto wrecking yards
  - Types of operation
  - Ability to dismantle or strip as needed
  - Condition of inventory
  - Membership in telephone pools

- Miscellaneous automotive businesses (Off-road vehicles and motor homes)
  - New versus used vehicles
  - Leases and contracts available (financing)
  - Repairs available
  - Floor costs

- Bicycle shops
  - Lines carried
  - Revenue from sales (new versus used)
  - Revenue from repairs
  - Clientele's age and income bracket
  - Income from accessories

- Bookstores
  - Breakdown of inventory (new versus used)
  - Sales (new versus used)
  - Magazines (new versus used)
  - Sales (hardcover versus paperback)
  - Sales of newspapers, specialty lines, and so on
  - Location
  - Proximity to competition and mall stores

- Building supplies and hardware stores
  - Sources of revenue (rental, wholesale, retail)
  - Sales by department
  - Type of lumber carried
  - Contracts with builders
  - History in the community
  - Brand lines (such as True Value, American Homes, and so on)

- Clothing stores
  - Type (women's, men's, children's, combinations)

- Specialties
- Sizes
- Fashions carried
- Lines (clothing, shoes, and so on)
- Price range
- Effect of competition on sales

- Drugstores and pharmacies
  - Revenue from prescriptions
  - Number of new and refill prescriptions
  - Insurance plans
  - Nonprescription sales
  - Hours of qualified pharmacist

- Flower/plant shops
  - Wire services (wire in and wire out)
  - Volume of weddings parties, holidays, and so on
  - Delivery services

- Furniture and appliance stores
  - Lines carried
  - Delivery service
  - Mark-up charges
  - Floor lines and costs
  - Service department

- Gift shops
  - Lines carried
  - Revenue from cards versus gifts
  - Dollar range of gifts
  - Major recognized brands (Hallmark, and so on)

- Miscellaneous retailers (cameras, sewing machines/vacuum cleaners, guns, pawn, lamps, toys, luggage, and so on)
  - Same information as for basic retail sales

- Motorcycle shops
  - Brands offered
  - Amount of repair work
  - Inventory of new and used bikes

- Inventory turnovers per year
- New versus used sales
- Financing available
- Advertising
- Floor planning costs
- Associated sales of accessories and clothing

- Music and video stores
  - Revenue from individual profit centers (sales and rentals)
  - Instruments and brands carried
  - Inventory turnover
  - Proximity to competition

- Pet shops
  - Types of animals carried
  - Number of fish tanks, bird cages and kennels filled or empty
  - Sources of healthy animals and supplies
  - Grooming income

- Television/electronics stores
  - Brands carried
  - Revenue from sales versus service
  - Outside services provided
  - Inventory breakdown (parts versus sets)
  - Authorized repair
  - Location and specialties versus competition

- Sporting goods stores
  - Lines carried
  - Number of steady customers, leagues, schools, businesses and so on
  - Types of sports represented by inventory
  - Major brands

Manufacturing and Distributing Businesses

- Manufacturing firms
  - Kinds of products
  - Value of work in progress
  - Method of acquiring jobs

- Bidding and negotiating methods
- Marketing methods
- Labor union representation
- Foreign and domestic competition
- State-of-the-art technology in use
- Long-term outlook for industry

- Distribution firms
  - Brands carried
  - Markup
  - Exclusive lines, territories, or areas
  - Percentage of profit
  - Number of accounts
  - Frequency of servicing accounts
  - Use of outside salespeople or manufacturing reps
  - Other services
  - Sales tax permits
  - Types of delivery services used
  - Products vended, type of equipment, location of machines, percentage paid to location, and tax permits needed

Franchises

- New franchises
  Price of business is established by franchisor

- Existing franchises
  Simply businesses that are grouped into specific categories and duplicated many times

  Franchises fall within almost every category previously outlined.

  Most franchise operations are in great demand, are highly recognizable, are profitable, and cost more to buy than a single operation.

  A franchise must be viewed simply as a business. All of the criteria used to purchase a business apply here as well. You can expect franchise fees, training, a transfer fee, a franchise agreement, and information from the franchisor about the franchise you are about to buy from the franchisee. Tracking this type of business may be a little easier than tracking a single operation.

A quality franchise is worth its weight in gold, as long as there is support from the franchisor and a history of success (for example, McDonald's, Jiffy Lube, Midas Mufflers, and many more).

6

A Buyer's Perspective

By now, as a well-educated buyer, you should have all of the tools necessary to logically assess a business you would love to own. But there's a little bit more I would like to share with you. The key to buying a business is within your own grasp. How well you understand this concept will determine your success in buying and negotiating for the business. You should understand a rule of thumb called the 90 percent rule:

Facts That Buyers Should Know About Buyers!

90% of all buyers are first-time buyers.

90% of all buyers will finance the purchase of their business.

90% of all buyers don't initially know what kind of business they want or what business best serves their needs.

90% of all buyers are terrified or uneducated in the initial stages of the business-buying process.

90% of all sales will be financed by the seller.

90% of the buyers will not buy the business that they saw first or that was advertised early in their buying process.

90% of the buyers will buy only when they are ready. You must learn your own motivations! What are your thoughts?

What Motivates a Buyer

Most people go into business

To have the satisfaction of being their own boss

To have more personal freedom

To make money or have more financial security

Don't make the mistake of trying only to match your income through the net profit of the business. Money is at best third on the list of motivations for buying a business.

A Business Is More Than Numbers

Remember, you are not buying numbers. You are buying

People

A location

A product or service

Equipment

History and experience

Customers

Opportunity

The Willing Buyer

See if the following list makes you smile, gets you angry—or at best, gets you in touch with reality:

The Ten Different Types of Buyers

The buyer who states that money is no problem

The serious and usually young buyer who is going to borrow money from wealthy Uncle Pete

The same serious, but not always young, buyer who is going to borrow all the money from the bank

The older buyer who is going to retire in a few years and wants a business to supplement retirement funds

The sometimes arrogant buyer who represents an investor group or is looking for a wealthy friend

The buyer with the need (unemployed)—a great person but with no money

The buyer who is out of touch with reality and thinks General Motors can be bought for a dollar

The buyer who tells you up front that he or she does nothing without an attorney, accountant, and banker

The buyer who knows what's for sale all over town—the proverbial "tire kicker" who has been looking forever

The Willing Buyer

The willing buyer has, in varying intensity, all of the following:

The strong desire to buy a business

The need or urgency to buy a business

The financial resources to buy a business

The ability to make his or her own decisions

Reasonable expectations of what ownership of a business can do

Be honest with yourself. If all five of the "willing" components aren't evident, you could be wasting your own time and future by looking into buying a business.

"Getting to Know You"

You may think that you can simply waltz in and "wow" the seller of the business that you might want to buy. You may have a wonderful personality, you may be smart, you may be a person who can "walk on water"—or at the very least walk in it up to your ankles. But don't get ahead of yourself.

I agree, self-confidence is a necessary and wonderful attribute to have, but so is the attribute of being prepared. It is imperative that you be prepared for a buyer interview. The sellers want to know who they are dealing with: friend or foe; buyer or looker; serious or not serious. Above all, sellers are looking for the person who has the ability to be a human being in a business environment.

You only get one chance to make a good first impression, so get in touch with yourself. Be able to explain to the seller some (if not all) of the following:

- Your needs
- Your background and/or work history
- Your likes and dislikes (be careful here)
- Your interests
- Your goals (business and personal)
- How long you have lived in the area
- Life status (married, single, family, and the like)
- Plans to operate the business on your own or with a partner or spouse
- Financial involvement of other people (who they are and their degree of involvement)
- How long you have been looking for a business, what you have seen, and why you haven't bought yet
- Your last or current job, your responsibilities, and your extent of authority
- Length of employment
- What you did and did not like about the job
- Whether you have ever owned a business, what type, and your level of success.
- What you enjoy doing in your spare time (sports, hobbies) and why
- What income you need from a business to maintain your lifestyle
- Amount of money you have to invest in a business (Does the amount include working capital? How liquid are the funds? How much time do you need to turn it into cash? Can this information be verified?)
- Whether you have applied for a loan yet (if you are depending on one) and who is providing it. Can this be verified?
- Why you want to buy a business—specifically, this business
- How soon you want or need to buy a business

Everything we've discussed thus far has helped you understand yourself, the process of analyzing a business thoroughly, ways to deal "people to people," and more. Now you have come to the most important point in this book: If you are sure, if you are confident, if you did your homework properly, then you are ready to buy your dream, your future.

Time to Make an Offer

The process of negotiating to buy a business is complex. These are the usual steps:
1. Offer by buyer (see Offer to Purchase)
2. Acceptance by seller or counteroffer (see Amendment/ Addendum to Offer to Purchase)
3. Acceptance by buyer or counter-offer
4. Acceptance by buyer and seller
5. Removal of contingencies (see Contingency Removal Form)
6. Completion of details
7. Closing (see Accomplish Prior to Closing)

Offer to Purchase

1. Buyer agrees to purchase from Seller the business described as follows, including all equipment, fixtures, goodwill, inventory, trademarks, trade names, and that business known as _____

   _____

   located at _____ .

2. The purchase price of $_____ shall be paid as follows:

   a. $_____ Deposit on the date of this agreement

   to be included in the down payment

   b. _____ Additional deposit upon acceptance by Seller to be included in the down payment

   c. _____ Balance of down payment due at the closing in cash or certified check

   $_____ Total down payment

   d. _____ Assumption of existing obligation payable as follows:

   $_____ /month (including ___% interest)

   e. _____ Assumption of existing obligation payable as follows:

   $_____ /month (including ___% interest)

    f.   _____ _____ Balance to Seller payable as follows:
        $_____ or more per month (including ___% interest)

    g. Additional terms: _____

                   _____

      $_____ Total purchase price

3. The closing shall take place at _____ o'clock __a.m. __p.m. on _____, 19___, at the office of _____; possession will be given at time of settlement; closing costs shall be shared equally by Buyer and Seller.

4. The full purchase price shall include marketable inventory of $_____ at Seller's cost. If the actual amount is more or less, the purchase price and down payment shall be adjusted accordingly. However, in no event shall the inventory amount exceed $_____.

5. The sales tax on fixtures and equipment, if any, shall be paid for by Buyer.

6. Seller warrants that, at the time physical possession is delivered to Buyer, all equipment will be in working order and premises will pass all inspections necessary to conduct such business.

7. Buyer and Seller agree to execute all documents necessary to consummate this transaction, including where applicable such documents as are necessary to comply with the Bulk Transfer provisions of the Uniform Commercial Code.

8. All deposits shall be held by an agreed-upon escrow agent, who, at its option, may hold Buyer's deposit check in an uncashed form until this agreement has been signed by Seller. Cashed deposits will be held in a noninterest-bearing account.

9. Buyer shall indicate his/her satisfaction with the assets and financial and other records of this business by initialing in the following space: ___. Upon acceptance of this agreement, Seller will immediately provide to Buyer verification of such information. Buyer's satisfaction shall be conclusively presumed after ___ days from receipt of Seller's verification unless contrary written notice is given to Seller or upon Buyer's assuming possession of the business, whichever is sooner. This document contains the entire understanding of the parties, and there are no oral agreements, understandings, or representations relied upon by the parties. Any modifications must be in writing and signed by both parties.

10. Seller warrants that he/she has a clear and marketable title to the business being sold, except as mentioned: _____ _____ _____

11. Seller shall deliver to Buyer a valid lease or assignment for a period of ___ years, first-year rental of $_____ per month, option of _____ .

12. The following adjustments and prorations shall be made at or before closing; rent, security deposits, _____, _____, _____, _____.

13. If Seller fails to accept this agreement by _____ o'clock ___a.m. ___p.m., _____, 19___, then Buyer may revoke this agreement.

BUYER AND SELLER INDIVIDUALLY ACKNOWLEDGE RECEIPT OF A COPY OF THIS AGREEMENT. BUYER HEREBY AGREES TO BUY AND SELLER HEREBY AGREES TO SELL ON THE TERMS SET FORTH ABOVE.

DATE_____   DATE_____

BUYER_____   CORPORATE NAME_____

_____

BUYER_____   SELLER_____

2. Acceptance by seller or counteroffer (see amendment/addendum to offer to purchase)

Amendment/Addendum to Offer to Purchase

I/We accept all of the terms and conditions of the attached offer to purchase, dated _____, on the business known as _____ except as follows:_____

_____

_____

_____

_____

_____

_____

_____

All other terms and conditions of the offer to purchase are to remain the same.

If Buyer fails to accept this offer by   o'clock   a.m. p.m.,   , 19 , then this counteroffer may be revoked by Seller and the deposit will be returned to Buyer.

All deposits shall be held by the broker or the agreed-upon escrow agent, who, at its option, may hold Buyer's deposit check in an uncashed form until this agreement has been signed by Buyer and Seller. Cashed deposits will be held in a noninterest-bearing account.

BUYER AND SELLER INDIVIDUALLY ACKNOWLEDGE RECEIPT OF A COPY OF THIS AGREEMENT.

DATED _____   DATED _____

BUYER _____ L.S. SELLER _____

BUYER _____ L.S. SELLER _____

3. Acceptance by buyer or counteroffer

4. Acceptance by buyer and seller

5. Removal of contingencies (see Contingenty Removal Form)

Contingency Removal Form

Date:_____

TO WHOM IT MAY CONCERN:

I/We, the undersigned Purchaser(s) of that certain business known as

_____

_____

_____ ,

located at _____ ,

hereby remove the contingencies on that certain Offer to Purchase

dated _____ ,

which reads _____

_____

_____

_____

_____

_____

_____

_____

_____

_____

_____

_____

_____

_____

All other terms and conditions of the Offer to Purchase are to remain
the same.

_____ L.S. Date _____

_____ L.S. Date _____

BY: _____

6. Completion of Details
7. Closing (See Accomplish Prior to Closing)

Accomplish Prior to Closing

1. _____Transfer telephone

2. _____Transfer electricity

3. _____Transfer water

4. _____Arrange for lease assignment

5. _____Open checking account

6. _____Arrange for new checks

7. _____Arrange for Visa and Mastercard

8. _____Apply for franchise license

9. _____Develop logo for business

10. _____Arrange for insurance

11. _____Order new stationery and envelopes

12. _____Arrange for Yellow Pages ad

13. _____Other _____

14. _____Other _____

15. _____Other _____

_____

_____

_____

_____

_____

_____

_____

_____

Negotiating the Sale

Always remember that you are buying the seller first and the business second. Make sure you have a complete understanding of the seller and confidence that you are getting all of the information honestly and accurately. Don't accept anything less than 100 percent honesty, backed up by verifiable data. The seller who gives you false or misleading information may get your hopes up initially, but in the long run, you will determine the truth and the deal will be blown. At that point, how could you ever feel safe in dealing with that type of individual again?

Let's review what you need to find out about yourself before making an offer:

What is your reason for buying a specific business?
Do you have the funds to buy the business?
What are your expectations about buying the business?
What are your expectations about owning the business?
Do you have a sense of urgency?

Now let's review what you need to know:

The business-buying process from beginning to end.
The dollars you need to get into the business.
The dollars you need to stay in the business.
Why the seller is selling.
The advantages and disadvantages of owning a business.

"I'm going to make you an offer your can't refuse." These famous words bring up images of the perfect deal. But real- life situations aren't as smooth as what we see in the movies or read in novels. Real life dictates that we double-check, if not triple-check, all contingencies. You can never be too careful.

Negotiating is nothing more than conferring with another so as to settle some matter. To negotiate the purchase of a business, you don't need the sophistication of persuasive powers of Henry Kissinger or the business acumen of Lee Iacocca. All you need is to be yourself. Your only objective is to close a deal that satisfies you and the seller. Yes, have the heart to understand that the seller wants to be treated fairly too. The closer you both come to a 50/50 deal, the happier you both will be and the faster you both will accomplish your goals. If you keep this precept in mind, you are less likely to fail. If either you or the seller gets a gut feeling that you are being taken advantage of, the deal will fail. The seller has to realize that you need to be able to buy the business, live out of the business, and make debt payments from the profits of the business. If this is not possible and the seller is squeezing more out of you than you can afford, then you're doomed to fail. On the other hand, the seller should have a reasonable expectation to derive a solid deal and to be rewarded for all the hard work and years of dedication that established the business you are buying and have deemed a worthwhile entity.

The Secrets of Making a Deal

The best tactic in negotiation is to remain reasonable and flexible. In addition, to be a successful negotiator you must

- Assume everything is negotiable.
- Be professional and never be afraid of saying no.
- Always leave room to negotiate.
- Never, ever accept the first offer.
- Never make the first negotiating movement.
- Always deal within a settlement range.
- Be able to show emotion and body movements to create doubt in the seller (this adds value to a concession).
- Insist on a deadline from the seller, but always allow a cushion in that deadline.
- Negotiate deadlines set by the seller
- Use the competition to your advantage when negotiating
- Get as much information as possible and give as little as possible.
- Ask many questions
- Avoid single-issue bargaining; discuss a broad range of issues.
- Answer questions with questions to avoid giving away information needlessly.
- Always assume that the seller is holding back some information.
- Always control your emotions.
- Never make the mistake of "knowing it all."
- Always assume that only two or three prime issues are involved.

- Use silence as a control and uncertainty as leverage.
- Try to create visual images in the seller to get an agreement.
- Avoid letting a weakness become a major issue.
- Concede slowly, if you must, and use the concession for "tradeoffs."
- Be willing to walk out.
- Always give reasons to help the seller come to an agreement.
- Know that power diminishes as time drags on.
- Always satisfy needs instead of wants so as to create a "win-win" situation for both sides.
- Be a good winner; always declare the seller the winner.

Your objective in negotiating is to create the best deal you can using your own style and approach. You may be able to close your deal over lunch or dinner. Or it may be many months before both of you are satisfied. Regardless of how long it takes or what transpires, remember this: Work for the best, but prepare for the worst.

The Art of Negotiating

To carry on a successful negotiation with a seller, you must be able to carry on a basic conversation. Is that a ridiculous statement to make? Not really. Think about the last time you met a person you didn't know or didn't know well. Did you feel totally comfortable with your overall conversation? Was the conversation substantial, or was it a "cocktail party," nowhere conversation? When dealing with a seller, you have to be able to get past the simple subjects, get to the meat of the situation, and do it in a manner that brings success and good feelings to both sides. If you think this is easy, role-play some negotiations with a friend. Ask him or her to assume the role of different people with different personalities. You're in for a real eye-opener.

Conversation is like magic. There are no real powers to accomplish a trick or to carry on a conversation. Magic is simply practice with the right apparatus and proper staging to allow the magician to amaze you. Conversation, and negotiation, is the proper preparation of the right words, using information you've gathered, to accomplish your goal.

Nothing leaves a poorer impression on a seller than an unprepared buyer. First, select a place for your negotiations that will provide privacy from interruption or distractions. If you are in an office, make sure the secretary is instructed to hold all calls, and state that you don't wish to be disturbed during your meeting. Review the information you have gathered for the meeting.

You will be the "master" of the negotiation. The attitude of the seller and the information you secure can be controlled by skillful questioning. In most negotiations two sellers are present: the real seller and the seller's "mask." Obviously, sellers want to present themselves in the most favorable light or at least as they feel you would like to see them. It's your job to distinguish between the real and the make-believe. Good questioning techniques can penetrate a seller's mask of behavior to discover the real person.

Before we discuss good questioning habits, it would be helpful to discuss the six most common errors in questioning that you can make. Try to
- Avoid questions that can be answered by only yes or no.
- Avoid unimaginative questions for which the seller has long since prepared answers.
- Avoid leading questions, which suggest the probable answer to the seller.
- Avoid questions or comments that are nonneutral and reveal your personal attitude.
- Avoid questions that both you and the seller know the answers to.
- Avoid questions that are unrelated to the task at hand.

Open-Ended Questioning

Your assignment is to ask questions that will help the seller express ideas and feelings totally, in an open and honest manner. The questions should be nondirective and simple. Such open-ended questions take a format like the following:
- Tell me about...
- I'd be interested in knowing...
- How do you feel about...
- To what do you attribute...

- I'm not certain I understand...
- Would you explain that in more detail?
- What do you mean by that?
- Tell me more about...
- Perhaps you could clarify...
- Has there been any opportunity to...
- What prompted your decision to...
- How did you happen to ...

Open-ended questioning is one of the best methods of carrying on an informative and friendly conversation while gathering vital information. Initially it may be difficult to ask open- ended questions, but with practice you will find it becomes second nature. The real reason for asking open-ended questions is to get substantial answers. Listen to what comes back to you. The reason we have two ears and one mouth is so we can listen twice as much as we talk. In negotiating, it would be to your advantage to talk only 10 percent of the time and listen 90 percent of the time. A wealth of knowledge and information can be gathered just by listening.

The Actual Sale

The acquisition of your business will have a long ancestry. All of the negotiations that you and the seller complete to your mutual satisfaction will form the basis of the final agreement.

Now it's time for the attorneys and accountants to try to formulate the final terms and conditions that will satisfy both you and the seller. Here is where you will get your maximum legal protection and tax benefits, defined around mutually agreed upon terms.

An attorney and an accountant could be brought in early, during the negotiations, to advise and resolve legal and tax matters. Later on, they may have to create or rearrange terms that you and the seller have agreed on. Resolve these matters early on so they won't have to be rejected later for legal or tax reasons. You know what you want and need to buy and run the business; the lawyers and accountants should be there only to advise on legal and tax matters, not on personal decisions.

Your attorney should obtain the following for you:
- Proper title to the business and its assets
- Legal protection against false representations from the seller, which could cause potential liabilities
- Indemnification from the seller

The seller's attorney will want the following for him or her:
- Tax advantages from the sale of the business
- Guarantees for the payment of debt service from you if the owner is financing
- Elimination of the seller's ties to the business that could create liability

These are the primary goals of you and the seller. The final contract of sale should address these issues and resolve any conflict.

The Offer to Purchase form included in this book only sets up the basis of the final contract. It should not be considered as the contract that will bind your deal. Your attorneys will hammer out a legal agreement based on the parameters of the Offer to Purchase.

A contract is a binding agreement between two or more persons or parties that is legally enforceable. It starts as a blank piece of paper that is written to the express wishes of you and the seller to accommodate your mutually agreed upon terms and conditions of sale. Contracts must be fully executed, and any changes have to be initialed by you and the seller. Amendments/addendums have to be fully executed also, and any changes must be initialed by you and the seller.

When a contract or offer to purchase is executed, an earnest money check must be submitted to an escrow company so as to open escrow. The earnest money check should be made out to the escrow company, not to the seller. Request a receipt for the deposit.

The escrow company will prepare the following documents:

Promissory note to seller
Chattel security agreement
UCC-1 Financing statement
Collection and payment information
Closing statement
Bulk transfer agreement
Additional forms that may be required

The seller must deliver to the escrow company before close of escrow, a complete equipment list and lease, if applicable. All conditions of a contract must be completed and delivered to the escrow company prior to closing escrow.

Both buyer and seller must attend the final closing of escrow. As the buyer, you must bring to the closing table certified funds for the balance owed. This check must be made out to the escrow company. To ensure a smooth closing, have the attorneys review all the documents prior to arriving at the closing. If there are any points to negotiate, do so prior to closing and not at the closing table.

If a stock sale is involved, review these aspects with your attorney. In a stock sale, you assume all assets of the businesses as well as all liabilities. You must review these legal aspects with your attorney. In addition, in a stock sale all of the stockholders must be present at the closing. They all must execute the contract. The following must also be at the closing: an up-to-date corporate minutes book, all stock certificates, the certificate book, up-to-date financials, and records of the corporation. All taxes prorated must be paid at close of escrow. The officers and directors of a corporation must resign their positions.

For an asset-only sale, the president and secretary of the corporation must sign any legal document of sale. The only document needed other than the list of assets is a corporate resolution.

The Agreement of Sale included here was for a corporation. It is an actual contract used to sell a business, with some pertinent data omitted to allow privacy. The business in question involved real estate as well as assets and inventory. It is an excellent example.

Agreement of Sale

THIS AGREEMENT, made this 22nd day of April 1991, by and between [name of business], a [name of state] corporation, located at [street address, city, state, ZIP], hereinafter called "Seller," and [buyer's corporate name], a [state] corporation, located at [full address], hereinafter called "Buyer";

WHEREAS, Seller represents that it is the owner of a certain [type of business] operated as [name doing business as] consisting of the following assets: land and premises known as [full address], trade name, goodwill, fixtures, equipment, personality, [type of license], and stock in trade; and

WHEREAS, Seller represents that it is presently conducting said [type of business] as aforesaid; and

WHEREAS, Seller desires to sell and Buyer desires to buy said [type of business] and assets, upon the terms and conditions hereinafter set forth;

NOW THEREFORE, in consideration of the mutual covenents herein contained, and each intending to be legally bound, the parties hereto agree as follows:

1. PURCHASE AND SALE

Buyer shall purchase from Seller and Seller shall sell to Buyer a certain [type of business] conducted under the trade name of [trade name] together with all real estate described in "Schedule A" attached hereto and made a part hereof, all furniture, furnishings, decorations, equipment, fixtures, and other personality set forth in "Schedule B" attached hereto and made a part hereof, trade names, goodwill, and [name of] license, free and clear of all debts, mortgages, security interests, liens, or encumbrances of any nature, except as set forth herein, which business shall be sold as a going concern.

2. PURCHASE PRICE

The purchase price shall be [dollar amount] payable as follows:
A. [dollar amount] deposit due upon the execution of the within Agreement of Sale by the parties.
B. [Dollar amount] due on [date of close of escrow].

  C. [Dollar amount] proceeds of a first loan to be obtained by Buyer.

  D. [Dollar amount] proceeds of a second mortgage loan to be granted by Seller.

All funds payable shall be in cash, certified, or treasurer's or bank check.

The purchase price shall be allocated as follows:

  A. Real estate .... $

  B. Personal property .... $

  C. Goodwill .... $

  D. Covenant not to compete .... $

  E. [Type of] license .... $ _____

      Total .... $

All deposit monies shall be held in an interest-bearing account by [name of escrow company], with interest to be applied to Buyer to [date of closing] and thereafter to Seller.

3. SETTLEMENT

Settlement shall be held at the offices of [name of escrow company], [full address], on [complete date] at [exact time], time being of the essence of this Agreement. At the time of settlement, Seller shall deliver to Buyer a bargain and sale deed, with covenants against grantors, acts, for the aforementioned land and premises and bill of sale for the aforementioned furniture, furnishings, decorations, equipment, fixtures, and personality. Seller, at the same time, shall assign and transfer all of its right, title, and interest in [type of] license, issued by [whomever].

4. POSSESSION

Possession hereunder shall be given to Buyer by Seller on [date], pursuant to the provisions of a certain Management Contract of even date, entered into by the parties hereto.

5. INVENTORY

Buyer shall buy, and Seller shall sell, all inventory and stock in trade located at the devised premises at the close of business for the business day [date], at Seller's cost of acquisition of said inventory and stock in trade. At Buyer's election, the sale price for said inventory and stock in trade may be paid in two equal monthly payments, including interest at [%] per annum, 30 days and 60 days, respectively, after [date]. Buyer may repay the balance on said price without penalty at any time.

6. FINANCING

The within Agreement of Sale is specifically contingent upon Buyer securing a first mortgage loan on the subject premise of, at least, [dollar amount] at an interest rate of no more than [%] per annum. Buyer shall immediately take application for said loan, and Seller agrees to cooperate in the securing of said loan.

Additionally, Seller agrees to grant a loan to Buyer of [dollar amount] at [%] per annum interest, payable in [number of] equal monthly payments of [dollar amount], secured by second mortgages with right of payment without penalty.

7. GOVERNMENT APPROVALS

The within Agreement of Sale is contingent upon the approval of the [name of specific government agency] of the transfer of [type of license] to Buyer and upon the receipt of all other governmental approvals, including a certificate of occupancy and mercantile license, if any, by Buyer necessary to the effectuation of the purposes of the within Agreement.

8. WARRANTY AS TO LICENSE

Seller warrants that it is the owner of [type of license] free and clear of all liens and encumbrances and further warrants that there are no violations pending against said license and that there shall be no violations pending against said license through the transfer of possession of the aforesaid [type of business].

9. CREDITORS

Seller agrees to furnish Buyer with a list of Seller's existing creditors, containing the names and business addresses of all such creditors with the amounts owed to each creditor and also the names and addresses of all persons who are known to Seller to assert claims against Seller, whether disputed or not. Such list shall be signed and sworn to, or affirmed by, Seller and shall be delivered to Buyer at least 15 days before [date], the date of settlement. Buyer agrees to preserve the list and a schedule of the personal property to be sold and purchased for a period of 6 months next following the date of the transfer of title and shall permit inspection of either or both and copying therefrom, at all reasonable hours, by any creditor of Seller; or in the alternative, shall file such list and schedule in the office of the Secretary of State of [name of state] as permitted by law. Buyer further agrees to give such notice to the creditors as is required and in the form and manner and within the time provided by law. Seller agrees to comply with all other terms and conditions of the [name of state] Bulk Sales Act.

10. ADJUSTMENTS

All adjustments, including but not limited to taxes, water, sewer, insurance, utilities, and [type of license] fees shall be made as of, and at, the time of transfer of possession.

11. OPERATION OF BUSINESS

Seller shall continue to operate the business during normal business hours, consistent with prior practice, and shall not effect any changes in its business. Seller shall use its best efforts to retain the services of its employees and to preserve the goodwill of its suppliers and patrons. The business and all assets mentioned herein, upon the transfer of possession, shall be in good condition, reasonable wear and tear excepted.

12. TITLE

The title to be delivered shall be marketable title, insurable by any reputable title company at ordinary rates, and shall be free and clear of all liens and encumbrances, including municipal liens and assessments. Seller warrants that there are no restrictions of record affecting the subject land and premises that would prohibit its use and/or occupancy as a [type of business].

13. ZONING

Seller warrants that the subject land and premises is presently zoned to permit a [type of business].

14. BANK ACCOUNTS AND RECEIVABLES

The parties hereto understand and agree that the sale and purchase herein provided for does not contemplate or include any bank accounts maintained by Seller or accounts receivable existing prior to the transfer of possession. All accounts payable existing prior to the transfer of possession shall be the obligation of the Seller.

15. TAXES

Seller shall be responsible for all federal, state, and local taxes, including payroll deductions due for the period prior to transfer of possession.

16. COVENANT NOT TO COMPETE

For a period of 10 years, and within the radius of 10 miles of the aforementioned subject land and premises, Seller nor any of its shareholders, officers, and directors, either directly or indirectly, shall own, manage, operate, or control or participate in the ownership, operation, management, or control of, or be connected with or have any interest in, as stockholder, director, officer, employee, agent, consultant, partner, or otherwise, in any [type of business] or other business engaged in the [type of product or products sold].

17. OFFSET

Should any of the warranties, representations, or obligations undertaken herein by the Seller to the Buyer be breached by Seller, resulting in financial loss to Buyer, Buyer may offset said financial loss against any obligations to Seller created pursuant to this agreement.

18. RISK OF LOSS

The risk of loss to assets aforementioned prior to settlement shall remain with Seller, and if said assets are destroyed by fire or any other casualty to the extent that the [type of business] cannot be operated in a normal fashion, then the within Agreement of Sale shall be null and void, with a return of deposit monies to Buyer. In the event said assets are damaged, but not to the extent that said business cannot be conducted in the normal fashion, it shall be the responsibility of Seller to either repair the damage or to make an appropriate adjustment in the sale price.

19. OUTSTANDING CONTRACTS

Seller warrants to Buyer that there are no outstanding contracts heretofore made by Seller or its predecessors, unless acknowledged by Buyer in writing, for [equipment, etc.] used in the aforesaid business, that would be binding on Buyer and agrees to hold Buyer harmless therefor and agrees to indemnify Buyer therefor.

20. PERSONAL PROPERTY

Seller warrants that all of the aforementioned furniture, furnishings, decorations, equipment, fixtures, and personality is owned by Seller free and clear of all encumbrances, liens, and security interests.

21. LICENSE TRANSFER

Buyer grees to make application to [name of specific agency] to transfer [type of license] to itself at Buyer's sole expense, including all required fees. Buyer shall make timely application for the transfer of said license, which application shall be the Buyer's sole responsibility, provided, however, that Seller agrees to cooperate and assist Buyer in the securing of said transfer.

22. INSPECTION OF ASSETS AND BOOKS

Buyer acknowledges that it has made a thorough and independent inspection of the aforesaid assets. Seller warrants ownership of said assets free and clear of liens and encumbrances and that all plumbing, heating, and electrical systems, as well as all fixtures, equipment, furnishings, furniture, and personality, shall be in good working order at the time of transfer and possession. Seller further warrants that the said premises and assets are in condition to pass all governmental inspections necessary to conduct the [type of business]. Buyer acknowledges that it has had an opportunity to examine the books and records of Seller regarding the aforesaid [type of business], which Seller warrants to be true and accurate, and that no representations have been made as to the amount of revenue that Buyer can anticipate upon taking possession of said business.

23. SURVIVAL OF TERMS OF AGREEMENT OF SALE

The provisions of the within Agreement of Sale shall survive settlement and any deed or bill of sale given hereunder.

24. BREACH OF AGREEMENT

Should the Seller breach the within Agreement of Sale, Buyer may elect to prosecute any action for damages and/or specific performance as allowed by law. Should Buyer breach the within Agreement of Sale, Seller may elect to prosecute any action for damages or to retain the deposit monies paid herein as liquidated damages.

Upon a failure of any of the contingencies set forth herein due to no fault of Buyer, Buyer, at its option, may elect to obtain the return of its deposit monies and declare the within Agreement of Sale null and void.

25. ENTIRE AGREEMENT

The within Agreement of Sale contains the entire agreement between the parties relating to the sale and purchase of said [type of business], and there exists no other verbal or other agreements modifying or changing the sale. All amendments hereto shall be in writing and executed by the parties.

26. APPLICABLE LAW

The within sale shall be construed according to the laws of the state of [name of state].

27. PARTIES IN INTEREST

All of the terms, conditions, and provisions herein contained shall inure to the benefit of, and shall bind, the parties hereto and their legal representatives, heirs, and assigns respectively.

28. HEADINGS

The headings contained within the Agreement of Sale are for reference purposes only and shall not affect, in any way, the meaning or interpretation of this Agreement of Sale.

29. SHAREHOLDER APPROVAL

Seller warrants that the sale and transfer of assets, as provided for herein, have been approved by its shareholders and board of directors.

IN WITNESS WHEREOF, THE PARTIES HERETO HAVE CAUSED THESE PRESENTS TO BE SIGNED BY THEIR PROPER CORPORATE OFFICERS AND CAUSED PROPER CORPORATE SEAL TO BE AFFIXED, THIS [DATE].

ATTEST: CORPORATION NAME OF BUYER
                                                    CORP. SEAL

_____   _____
SECRETARY OF CORP.   PRESIDENT OF CORP.

ATTEST: CORPORATION NAME OF SELLER
                                                    CORP. SEAL

_____   _____
SECRETARY OF CORP.   PRESIDENT OF CORP.

Guaranty by Shareholders

The undersigned shareholders of [corporate name of buyer] and [corporate name of seller] covenant, represent, and guarantee that each of the representations of their respective corporations are true and accurate to the best of their knowledge, information, and belief.

[CORPORATE NAME OF BUYER]:   **DATED:**

By:_____   _____
      [Name], Shareholder

By:_____   _____
      [Name], Shareholder

[CORPORATE NAME OF SELLER]:

By:_____   _____
      [Name], Shareholder

By:_____   _____
      [Name], Shareholder

Schedule "A"

ALL THAT CERTAIN tract or parcel of land and premises situated in the City of [name of city], County of [name of county], and State of [name of state], being more particularly described as follows:

BEGINNING at the intersection of the centers of [name of street] and [name of cross-street]; thence along [specifically name directions and degrees to precisely locate said business as a geographical entity].

Containing [precise number of acres].

IN COMPLIANCE with [specific land definition], on the Tax Map of [name of city].

SCHEDULE "B"

[This schedule, on its own page, lists all of the hard assets of the business. Hard assets can be defined as equipment. The list must be specific and define which department of the business each item belongs in and its total description. Identification numbers will thoroughly identify the assets.]

The other document in this section is an actual example of a contract used to sell a sole proprietorship. No land and very few hard assets were involved. The business had a large customer base and a high cash flow. These two reasons were enough for the buyer to make an offer. Since the buyer had no money to put down, the seller agreed to the terms and conditions in the contract. This is a wonderful example of how a buyer and seller with the proper amount of reasonability and flexibility can construct and consummate a business deal. As with the previous contract, the names of the parties and of the business are omitted to preserve privacy.

Agreement of Purchase and Sale

This agreement is entered and effective as of [date] by and between [buyer's name] and [seller's name].

RECITALS

[Seller] owns an unincorporated business doing business as [name of business]. [Buyer] desires to purchase from [Seller] on the terms and conditions specified herein. Accordingly, the parties agree as follows:

1.0 Payments

1.1 [Buyer] agrees to pay [Seller] [dollar amount] per calendar month on the first day of each calendar month, beginning [date] and continuing until [date]. Said [dollar amount] shall be allocated [dollar amount] to interest and [dollar amount] to consulting services.

1.2 On or before [date], [Buyer] shall pay [dollar amount] to [Seller]. Said [dollar amount] and interest thereon of [dollar amount] shall be paid in accordance with the note attached to this agreement as Exhibit C, which note is hereby incorported into this agreement.

1.3 The balance of [dollar amount] due [Seller] shall be payable over [number of years], with [%] per annum interest, in accordance with the note attached to this agreement as Exhibit A, which note is hereby incorported into this agreement.

1.4 Any sales tax due on this sale shall be the responsibility of [Buyer].

1.5 Any accounts receivable of [name of business] existing on the date of this agreement shall remain the property of [Seller], and [Buyer] shall remit any amounts collected on said receivables after taking possession to [Seller].

2.0 Assets Being Purchased

2.1 All of the tangible assets listed in Exhibit B are included in the sale by [Seller] to [Buyer], and both parties hereby agree that the values shown next to each listing are the fair market value for each listing.

2.2 The trademarks [doing business as] are included in the purchase price, and [Seller] hereby agrees to take all actions necessary to transfer ownership of said copyrights to [Buyer].

2.3 [Buyer] and [Seller] hereby agree to cooperate with [name], CPA, in preparing IRS Form 8594 and doing the allocation of asset values required by IRS Code section 1060.

2.4 All liabilities of [name of business] as of the date of this agreement, whether known or unknown, fixed or contingent, shall be the sole responsibility of [Seller].

3.0 Closing

3.1 The closing of this transaction shall take place at [time] on [date]. At said time, [Seller] shall give possession of [name of business] and its assets to [Buyer].

3.2 It is hereby agreed that a bulk sale notice shall be given as soon as possible. [Seller] agrees to cooperate in any way necessary for the giving of said notice and further agrees to assume responsibility for payment of any claims arising before [date] asserted as the result of said notice.

3.3 It is agreed that [Seller] shall be entitled to have a UCC-1 filing done on the assets listed in Exhibit B, to secure his interest under this agreement, and [Buyer] agrees to cooperate fully in doing said filing.

3.4 The business has recently been required to move, and certain expenses have been incurred in making said move. The parties hereto agree to split evenly the costs of said move, up to a total of [dollar amount]. If, for any reason, the expenses of said move exceed [dollar amount], then the parties hereto hereby agree to negotiate in good faith as to who should pay the expenses in excess of [dollar amount].

4.0 Consulting Services

4.1 [Seller] hereby agrees to remain available to consult with [Buyer] on an as-needed basis through [date], by telephone and in person, upon reasonable notice by [Buyer]. After [date], and before [date], [Seller] hereby agrees to remain available to consult with [Buyer] on an as-needed basis by telephone, provided, however, that said consulting availability shall not exceed [number] hours per month unless the parties hereto shall further agree as to such additional services. The parties hereby agree that if [Buyer] should make the payment specified in section 1.2 before [date], then [Seller] shall have no further consulting obligations under this section as of the date of said payment and [Buyer] shall have no further duty to pay [Seller] for his consulting services.

4.2 [Seller] shall be paid the amount specified in 1.1 for his consulting services during the term specified in 4.1.

5.0 Convenant Not to Compete

5.1 The parties agree that because [Buyer] is purchasing the goodwill of [Seller] and because competition by [Seller] in the field of providing [type of specific business] would substantially detract from the value of the business to [Buyer], enforcement of and compliance with the covenant not to compete described by this section is essential to effectuate the purpose of this agreement. {Seller] agrees not to provide specific assistance nor own any ownership interest in any business providing such services, in competition with the business, after [date], within [geographic boundaries], for a period of five years after [date].

6.0 Miscellaneous

6.1 [Seller] agrees that all business data pertaining to [business] to which he has access before or after [date] constitutes proprietary information purchased by [Buyer] pursuant to this agreement and will constitute trade secrets owned by [Buyer]. Accordingly, [Seller] will not disclose such materials to any third party without the prior express written consent of [Buyer].

6.2 Should any litigation be commenced between the parties to this agreement or the rights and duties of either party in relation thereto, the party prevailing in such litigation shall be entitled, in addition to such other relief as may be granted, to a reasonable sum as and for attorney fees in such litigation. The amount of said fees shall be determined by the Court in such litigation or in a separate action brought for that purpose. The parties expressly agree that the [name of court] of the state of [name of state] for the county of [name of county] shall be the proper forum for any judicial proceedings originating between the parties and resulting from this agreement.

6.3 Any and all notices or other communication required or permitted by this agreement or by law to be served on or given to either party hereto, [Buyer] or [Seller], by the other party to this agreement shall be in writing and shall be deemed duly serviced when personally delivered to the party to which such notices or communications are directed, or in lieu of such personal service, when deposited in the United States mail, first-class postage prepaid, to the addresses shown below:

[Buyer's full name and address]

[Seller's full name and address]

6.4 This agreement constitutes the sole and only agreement between the parties respecting the business and correctly sets forth the obligations of the parties to each other as of its date. Any agreements or representations respecting the business and its sale to [Buyer] not expressly set forth in this agreement are null and void.

6.5 This agreement shall be binding on and shall inure to the benefit of their heirs, executors, administrators, successors, and assigns of the parties hereto.

6.6 This agreement may not be assigned.

6.7 Any and all commissions due on the transaction contemplated by this agreement shall be the sole responsibility of [Seller].

6.8 Beginning with [month and year] and ending with [month and year], [Buyer] shall provide [Seller] with copies of the monthly bank statements and the monthly general ledger for the business for the preceding month by the fifteenth day of the following month. During the said period, [Buyer] shall also provide [Seller] with quarterly profit and loss statements within thirty days of the end of each calendar quarter, beginning with the period from [month and year] to [month and year].

6.9 If [Buyer] shall default on the obligation hereunder, then, in addition to any other remedies [Seller] may have under this agreement, [Buyer] shall surrender any pertinent data in [Buyer's] possession within three days of the receipt of written notice from [Seller] demanding the surrender of said data. Executed on this date first set forth above.

_____   _____
      [Seller]   [Buyer]

Exhibit A

Promissory Note

[dollar amount]   [city, state]   [date]

In installments as herein stated, I promise to pay [Seller], in order, at [full address], the sums of [dollar amount], with interest from [date] on unpaid principal at the rate of [%] per annum; principal and interest payable in installments of [dollar amount] per month on the first day of each calendar month beginning on the first day of [month and year] and continuing until said principal and interest have been paid.

Each payment shall be credited first on interest then due and the remainder on principal; and interest shall thereupon bear like interest as the principal, but such unpaid interest so compounded shall not exceed an amount equal to simple interest on the unpaid principal at the maximum rate permitted by law. Should default be made in payment of any installment of principal or interest when due, the whole sum of principal and interest shall become immediately due at the option of the holder of this note. Principal and interest are payable in lawful money of the [country]. If action be instituted on this note, I promise to pay such sum as the Court may fix as attorney's fees.

_____

[Buyer]

Exhibit B

Inventory and Assets
[complete itemized list of all inventory and assets.]

Exhibit C

Promissory Note

[dollar amount]   [city, state]   [date]

[similar to Exhibit A, except that it reflects the payment of a lump-sum balloon payment due on an exact date and an additional monthly payment of an exact amount for a period of twelve months—all other portions exactly as in Exhibit A.]

As the buyer of a business, you are experiencing real life at its best or its worst. Use all of the information in this book as if the future of you and your family were at stake. If you do your homework and don't short-circuit any of the steps, you will be able to construct and consummate a successful business purchase of your own.

This Is Important.

You are entering into an honorable agreement to purchase a living, breathing entity called a business. It is someone's "baby," someone's lifelong dream. That person is now entrusting you with the responsibility of carrying on that dream. In your dealings and negotiations for this business, understand well that the deal has to be as good for you as it is for the seller. You both must be convinced all the way to the closing table that you are both getting a good deal. It must be as close to a 50/50, or "win-win" situation as possible, or the deal won't close. If either you or the seller becomes more demanding during negotiations, if either the buyer or the seller feels the rope tightening around his or her neck, I guarantee you that the business will not close and the parties will walk away. Be fair, be reasonable—and expect the same from the other side.

Remember that you are capable of getting what you want. Don't continue to trade your time working for someone else for limited wealth (your salary). I promise you, as long as you are working for someone else you are never going to be able to earn enough or accumulate enough to create real wealth. Your employer is always going to maximize its benefit by limiting yours. This is a basic law of economics. The solution is to put the mechanics of wealth to work for you by seeking out and "safely" buying your own business.

I wrote this book to help you. If you would like to discuss any aspects of buying a business or have any questions at all, please feel free to contact me to arrange a private consultation at your convenience. Write directly to

Martin H. Bloom, President
International Business Marketing
4157 Vantage Avenue, Suite 1100
Studio City, California 91604
Or Telephone 818-506-0092

A Glossary of Terms
Often Used in Business Transactions

The ever-changing world of business sales presents a constant challenge to stay current and up to date. Over the years, an array of terms and concepts have become a part of that world. New ways of financing and major changes in tax laws have contributed to this growing list.

This glossary of terms and expressions will help you find your way through today's business language. Each entry is clearly and concisely defined and presented for your use. Whether you are a first-time buyer or a seasoned business buyer, you will find this alphabetical guide to business terminology extremely helpful.

The key to business communication is a common language. Business decisions can be chaotic when made on the basis of misunderstood terms and terminology. This glossary is designed for those who want to improve their language skills and have an up-to-date understanding of business concepts and terminology.

ACCELERATION CLAUSE

Clause in a mortgage giving the lender the right to call all sums owing the lender to be immediately due and payable upon the anniversary of an event, normally a default.

ACCEPTANCE

Act of agreeing to an offer, resulting in a binding contract.

ADDENDUM

Document adding something not previously covered to a contract.

AFFIDAVIT

Written statement signed and sworn to by the affiant before any officer authorized by law to administer oaths.

AGREEMENT OF SALE

Written agreement (document) whereby the "buyer" agrees to buy certain property and the "seller" agrees to sell such property under the specific terms and conditions set forth.

AMENDMENT

Document changing something in a contract previously agreed to.

AMORTIZATION

Gradual extinction of a monetary obligation by periodic contributions together with the payment of interest on the debt.

APPRECIATION

Increase in the value of property due to economic or other causes that may prove to be temporary or permanent.

ARBITRATION

Method of resolving disputes, claims, or matters between parties by a person or organization chosen by the parties; normally results in a fairly quick decision or resolution; usually a practical alternative to litigation, with its normally long delays and great expense.

ASSIGNMENT

Transfer in writing of an interest in property or other thing of value from one person to another.

ASSUMPTION OF NOTE

One party's agreement to totally relieve another party of personal liability, by creating a new note and terminating the original.

BALLOON PAYMENT

Final installment payment on a note that is substantially greater than the preceding installment payments and that pays the note in full.

BILL OF SALE

Written document transferring to a buyer the title to personal property.

BOND

Generally an obligation under seal.

BOOK VALUE

Value of an asset as carried on the books of a business, usually computed as the original cost plus improvements less depreciation.

BREACH OF CONTRACT

Failure of a party to a contract to perform any or all of his or her obligations under the contract.

BULK SALES LAW

Law requiring the purchaser of any commercial business to demand the names and addresses of all creditors of the seller; the buyer is then given a period of time (to be arranged) before closing (date of transfer of the business) to notify the creditors of the proposed purchase.

BULK TRANSFER LAW

Law protecting the interests of creditors of a business being sold.

BUSINESS EXPENSE

Money expended for any purpose to conduct business (rent, utilities, maintenance, etc.).

BUSINESS TRADE NAME

Company name by which a certain business is known.

CHATTEL

Personal property, such as household goods, stock, equipment, fixtures, etc.

CLOSING STATEMENT

Accounting of funds made by and for the seller and buyer separately and required by law to be made at the completion of every transaction, an exact copy of which is given to buyer and seller; usually prepared by an escrow agent.

COLLATERAL

Deposit of something of value to guarantee the payment of an indebtedness.

CONSIDERATION

Anything of value given or promised by each party to a contract to the other in order to make it legally binding; may be money, services, promises to perform, or other undertakings required by either party to the contract.

CONTINGENCIES

Possible future happenings that will affect the rights or obligations of contracting parties.

CORPORATION

Legal entity organized by one or more persons and treated by the law as an individual or unit with its own rights and obligations, all distinct and apart from those of the persons owning or operating it.

COST OF GOODS

Amount of money spent on inventory in order to conduct business for a certain period of time.

COVENANT NOT TO COMPETE

Agreement made part of the purchase contract in which the seller promises not to enter into a similar business for a specified period of time in a designated area.

CREDITOR

Person to whom debt is owed by another person, who is called the debtor.

DBA (Doing Business As)

Assumed designation used by individuals operating a business (for example, John Adams dba XYZ Corp.).

DEPRECIATION

Loss in value brought about by deterioration through ordinary wear or by operation of law.

DURESS

Unlawful constraint exercised upon a person whereby he or she is forced to do something against his or her will.

EARNEST MONEY RECEIPT

Receipt for a down payment, an offer to purchase, a contract of sale, or a contract to sell that sets down the time and method of closing.

ENCUMBRANCE

Claim, lien, charge, or liability attached to and binding upon real or personal property, such as a judgment, unpaid taxes, or a right of way; usually diminishes the value of the property in the hands of the owner and yet does not necessarily deprive him or her of the title thereto or use thereof nor of the power to convey or transfer the same.

EXCLUSIVE LISTING

Business broker's authority to sell a business and right to receive a commission (from the seller) no matter who sells the business.

FIXTURES AND EQUIPMENT

All fixed assets or other land and buildings of a business.

FRINGE BENEFITS

Items or expenses deducted as business expenses but not necessary to run or conduct the business.

GOODWILL

Favor or prestige that a business has acquired beyond the mere value of what it sells, which is the basis for additional dollar value.

GROSS PROFIT

Gross sales less (minus) the cost of goods.

GROSS SALES

Total amount of income that a business generates in a designated period of time (monthly, quarterly, etc.).

INDEMNIFY

To secure against loss or damage; to make reimbursement to one for a loss already suffered.

INTEREST

Money paid for the use of funds; rent paid for the use of money; return on investment (ROI).

INVENTORY

Items or articles the company uses to produce a product or sells to earn its profit.

IRREVOCABLE

Incapable of being recalled or resolved; unchangeable.

LEASE

Legal document by which the owner of a property gives possession of it to a second party for a specified period of time and for a specified rent, setting forth the conditions upon which the tenant may use and occupy the property.

LEASE WITH OPTION TO PURCHASE

Lease in which the lessee has the right to purchase the real property for a stipulated price at or within a stipulated time.

LEASEHOLD

Property held under tenure of lease; property consisting of the right of use and occupy by the virtue of a lease agreement; lessee's (tenant's) interest in a title.

LEASEHOLD IMPROVEMENTS

Any article or fixture that is attached to land or building, thereby becoming a part of said land or building.

LEASEHOLD INTEREST RIGHTS

Difference between actual rent and economic rent over the remaining period of the lease.

LEGAL DESCRIPTION

Precise identification of real property.

LIEN

Special encumbrance or charge against property whereby the property is made security for the payment of debt or such charge as a judgment, mortgage, or taxes; asset to the property's owner that may be assigned.

MARKET VALUE

Highest price that a buyer, willing but not compelled to buy, would pay and lowest price that a seller, willing but not compelled to sell, would accept.

MISREPRESENTATION

Statement contrary to fact when made with intent to deceive.

MORTGAGE

Written instrument recognized by law by which real property is pledged to secure a debt or obligation; lien on real property.

NEGOTIABLE

Capable of being negotiated; assignable or made transferable in the ordinary course of business.

NET INCOME

Income from a property or a business after expenses have been deducted; generally, gross income less operating expenses.

NET LEASE

Lease in which the tenant pays not only the rent but also certain agreed-upon property expenses, such as taxes and maintenance.

NOTE

Written document that acknowledges a debt and promises to pay on specified terms.

OPTION

Written agreement granting to a party the exclusive right, during a stated period of time, to buy or obtain control of property on specified terms but without any obligation of such party actually to do so.

PERCENTAGE LEASE

Lease of property in which the rental fee for its use is measured by or dependent on the volume of business transacted by the lessee, usually an agreed-upon percentage of the gross receipts of the lessee.

PERSONAL PROPERTY

Any property that is not real property.

POINTS

Loan fee exacted by the lender from the seller (sometimes the buyer) at the time the loan is made, based on the amount of the loan.

POWER OF ATTORNEY

Instrument authorizing a person to act as the agent of the person granting it: a general power authorizing the agent to act generally in behalf of his or her principal; special power limiting the agent to a specific or particular act.

PREPAYMENT CLAUSE

Statement in a mortgage permitting partial or full payment of the debt prior to the due date, often requiring a penalty payment if the clause is exercised.

PRORATION OF TAXES

Division of taxes between seller and buyer equally or proportionately to the time of closing on the property.

RELEASE

Relinquishment of some right or benefit to a person who usually and already has some interest in the property.

REPLACEMENT COST

Cost of replacing a property or compensating for its loss or destruction.

STATUTE OF FRAUDS

State law providing that certain contracts—such as the sale of real property, a lease of real property for more than one year, or a broker's authorization to sell a business or real estate—must be in writing in order to be enforceable.

SUBORDINATION

Act of making an encumbrance secondary or junior to another lien.

TERMS

Basic arrangements and provisions made on a mortgage or in a contract.

TITLE

Evidence of ownership that refers to the quality of the estate; right, interest, or estate in real property.

VOID

Having no force or enforceable effect.

PUBLISHER'S NOTE

ADDITIONAL COPIES OF **BUSINESS BUYING BASICS** may be purchased at your local bookstore, or direct from **Robert Erdmann Publishing** by sending your check or money order for $12.95, plus $2.00 postage and handling (California residents add 8¹/₂% tax) to: **Robert Erdmann Publishing, 810 W. Los Vallecitos Blvd., Suite 210, San Marcos, CA 92069.** Also, write this address for complete **Robert Erdmann Publishing Catalog.**

ATTENTION: SCHOOLS AND CORPORATIONS

BUSINESS BUYING BASICS and other books from **Robert Erdmann Publishing** are available at quantity discounts with bulk purchase for educational, business, or sales promotional use. For information, please write or call: Special Sales Department, Robert Erdmann Publishing, 810 W. Los Vallecitos Blvd., Suite 210, San Marcos, CA 92069, Phone — 619/471-4848, FAX — 619/471-5044.

Index